THE NEUTROPENIC COOKBOOK

OVER 100 TASTY, LOW-MICROBIAL DINNER RECIPES

FOR LOW IMMUNE SYSTEMS

AND POST-CHEMOTHERAPY

Alison Coates

Copyright© Alison Coates 2023
No part of this publication may be reproduced, copied, or transmitted except with the written permission of the author

Disclaimer:
The information provided in this book is intended for informational purposes only. The author is not a doctor, nutritionist, or dietician and has no medical or culinary training. The information shared is based on the author's own experiences and research. The author is not responsible or liable for any health issues that might result from following the published recipes. The content within the book is not intended as medical diagnosis or treatment and should not be considered a substitute for professional medical expertise. If the reader thinks they have any type of medical condition, they should always seek professional advice.

Praise for 'The Neutropenic Cookbook'

"What a wonderful cookbook! It's exactly what's needed after HSCT - a practical guide to help people balance the need to eat healthily while not risking infection during the recovery period. The recipes are simple and practical, and mean you'll have no problem eating well." *Caroline Wyatt, Journalist – underwent HSCT in 2017*

"I became familiar with Alison Coates through her efforts to educate patients with multiple sclerosis (MS) about hematopoietic stem cell transplantation (HSCT). So many of my patients have asked "Why aren't people standing on roof tops shooting about HSCT for MS?" With proper patient selection and the proper regimen, the outcome is stunning, and patients have improved and remained in treatment-free remissions for decades. Yet the medical community has remained oddly quiet, often not informing patients of this option. Alison decided to do something about this void by starting a patient education and self-help charity called AIMS. She did this by volunteering her time. It is her passion to awaken our medical system. While one should refer to their physician or nutritionist for medical advice, this book plays an important intermediary role to help facilitate questions and discussions between medical profession and patients. The medical community is also starting to recognize that our diet affects our gut microbiome, that is the bacteria in our gut, and that the microbiome can affect our health. Within the medical community, we are just beginning to understand that healthy diets may play a more important role in preventing some diseases and in affecting longevity. I found her recipes so surprisingly delicious that I will be trying some myself. I write this in admiration of her (and all my patients and the patients who contributed to her recipes) and encourage patient involvement and education about their diseases and life-options." *Professor Richard Burt MD, Filbright Scholar Scripps Health care La Jolla, California, Author of "A Stem Cell Journey, Curing Multiple Sclerosis, Scleroderma, and Autoimmune Diseases with Hematopoietic Stem Cell transplantation"*

"Alison's cookbook is a testament to the self-help, self-management movement sweeping the chronic disease field. Her book will educate anyone affected by a low immune system or undergoing chemotherapy treatment about the importance of diet in preventing at least one source of infection, food. Her recipes are nutritious and tasty, making adhering to a neutropenic diet less difficult." *Gavin Giovannoni (Professor of Neurology at Barts and the London School of Medicine and Dentistry)*

"As HSCT for MS moves to centre stage in treatment pathways it is important that patients and carers are well informed of what to expect and what they can safely do. Books like this address a significant unmet need in giving important help and guidance alongside that given by the clinical teams. The remit goes beyond MS as the principles of safe but nutritious food is applicable to other situations where the immune system can be compromised. I congratulate Alison for her tireless efforts in pulling this together alongside her continued advocacy for patients wishing to undertake HSCT. I do hope that readers find it a helpful adjunct to advice and guidance from their clinical teams." *Majid Kazmi (Consultant Haematologist King's College Hospital and London Bridge)*

For James

The book is dedicated to my amazing husband James, for whom HSCT was life-changing, and of whom I am so very proud; you bring sunshine and laughter to my days, and we have fought this battle side by side. Also, to my lovely daughters Rebecca and Lucy for being my guinea pigs (along with James), my wonderful Mum for instilling a love of cookery (and language) in me from a young age, and to my sister, Caroline, for her constant support. Thank you also to the trustees at AIMS, past and present, and friends who have supported me on this project - you know who you are. The book is also dedicated to all MS and HSCT warriors, but particularly to our sadly missed former trustee Mark Rye, and to the late Paul George who was also very supportive of AIMS. Also to Luke Callinan who is bravely battling this disease along with so many others. A big thank you goes to my cousin Nadege for tirelessly testing all my recipes, proofreading, and contributing many of the beautiful photos you see in this book, and to Gwen Higgs and Robert Douglas-Fairhurst for proofreading and for being wonderful advocates for HSCT.

FOREWORD

This book, as the title suggests, is a collection of recipes suitable for anyone following a neutropenic diet. That could be someone with a low immune system, for whatever reason, or someone who is recovering from cancer treatment. In this case, the recipes were a labour of love for my husband James, who was diagnosed with Multiple Sclerosis in 2011, and underwent a Haematopoietic Stem Cell Transplant (HSCT) in the summer of 2016, leaving him with a weakened immune system for some months. As a keen cook, I wanted to ensure plenty of variety for James in his diet while he was recovering, and that is how this collection came about.

While there are lots of resources detailing what should be avoided on a neutropenic diet, I couldn't find much in the way of actual recipes - particularly dinners - that were specifically suited to someone following this regime, and so I decided to develop my own collection. I noticed that other people seemed to be keen to find such recipes too, and so I started the Facebook group "Neutropenic Recipes and Advice Post-HSCT" to share ideas and to promote this book prior to its being published. At the time of publication, the group now has over 1500 members, with new people joining daily.

Ultimately, however, this really is just a collection of home-cooked, tasty, family meals, and recipes passed down from one generation to the next. If you are not on a restrictive diet, these recipes are suitable for just about anyone. The neutropenic diet itself is straightforward - it is a diet designed to limit the risk of food-borne bacteria; you may also see it referred to as a 'low-microbial' diet. There are more than 5.5 million cases of food poisoning reported in the U.K. every year. In America this figure is estimated to be closer to 48 million, with 128,000 hospitalisations and 3,000 deaths every year. It stands to reason that anyone with a weakened immune system, as is the case following HSCT and chemotherapy is not only going to be at greater risk of food poisoning but is also going to find any infection harder to fight off. For this reason, it is critical that anyone needing to follow a neutropenic diet practises safe food handling, and cooks and selects food in a way that minimises the risk to their health.

Since starting this journey, I have noticed several questions that seem to come up regularly. In the following pages, I hope that you will find answers to those questions, as well as an easy-to-follow table detailing foods to be avoided, as well as acceptable, safe choices.

Finally, wherever possible I have included tips to allow you to modify the recipes for a particular diet. Prior to his transplant, James followed a no dairy/gluten/red meat diet and our eldest daughter, who suffers from a different chronic condition, follows a gluten free diet, so there are some suggested relevant recipe hacks throughout the book too.

I'm absolutely a home cook, not a chef. I enjoy experimenting with textures and flavours, and I'm always tasting as I go. This is one of the reasons I don't particularly like baking - it's very regimented and precise! And easy to get wrong! I like being able to be flexible, so do taste as you go and adapt as you see fit. That's what I do! Don't be afraid to use jars and tinned produce on this eating plan - they're very safe because they've been heat-treated and are shelf-stable, so while I usually advocate cooking from scratch, the jars and tins are your friend during this period! In many cases you'll see a very simplified method and list of ingredients - post-HSCT cooking shouldn't be too complex. The book goes hand in hand with our charity, set up to help people with MS and Autoimmune Disease -AIMS (Auto Immune and Multiple Sclerosis).

Our website can be found at: www.aimscharity.org

A proportion of the profits raised from the sale of this book will go to the AIMS charity to support ongoing and new projects. Thank you for your support in buying this book.

CONTENTS

1. Autoimmune Disease PP13-18

2. What Is Multiple Sclerosis? PP18-25

3. HSCT for MS and Autoimmune Disease PP26-29

4. AIMS Charity PP30-33

5. The Basics of The Neutropenic Diet PP35-36

6. FAQ About The Neutropenic Diet PP37-42

7. The Neutropenic Diet in Detail PP43-49

8. The Recipes PP51-215

9. Conversion Tables & Quick Swaps For Different Diets PP216-218

Autoimmune Disease

In order to understand what an autoimmune disorder is, and what it isn't, you need to understand how your immune system operates. The immune system is the human body's defence system. It helps you fight off everything from the common cold to a variety of infectious diseases. When the body detects an antigen, an immune response is caused. For the immune system to operate effectively, it must be able to tell the difference between what is a part of the body and what isn't; specifically, recognising a foreign antigen and a self-antigen. If something impacts on the immune system's ability to do this, an autoimmune disorder may develop.

Autoimmune diseases can affect various areas of the body and, with 80 different autoimmune diseases, they can be incredibly difficult to diagnose. Autoimmune diseases can have a range of symptoms. Signs and symptoms of autoimmune disorders include joint pain, recurring fever, and skin issues, to name just a few.

What Causes Autoimmune Disease?

If you develop an autoimmune disease, your body will be attacking itself. The immune system is incredibly complicated, made up of organs and cells that work as a shield to protect your body from foreign invaders. When the immune system is no longer able to recognise what is a threat and what is not, it creates auto- antibodies which damage normal cells. While this occurs, T- lymphocytes (cells that are supposed to keep the autoimmune system in order) begin to fail as well, leading to an all-out attack.

This is essentially what causes autoimmune disease, but the root cause of the defect in immune systems is largely unknown. However, theories include everything from viruses, trauma, and chemical irritants, to drugs and environmental issues The autoimmune disease symptoms checklist is not an exhaustive one. One of the issues with using something like an autoimmune disorders' symptoms checker is that symptoms vary depending on the type of autoimmune disorder you have. Signs and symptoms of autoimmune disorders can also be mistaken for other conditions, and some seem to be correlated. For instance, studies have suggested that autoimmune hepatitis and MS share an inflammatory origin. This is particularly interesting as, while one is an autoimmune liver disease, the other impacts on the nerve cells and spinal cord. Other potential symptoms and health problems may include hair loss, numbness or a tingling feeling, difficulty concentrating, swelling and rashes. Many symptoms are also unique to a particular disorder - such as blood in your stool, often present in patients who have Crohn's disease autoimmune disorder. For most autoimmune diseases, symptoms will flare up and then subside. You may experience remissions where symptoms disappear completely, but this does not mean that your autoimmune disease has gone away or is cured.

Tests for Autoimmune Diseases

An autoimmune disease test can be irritating and time consuming for patients. No single test can tell you whether you have an autoimmune disorder, and even testing positive may not immediately provide you with information on which autoimmune disease you have. As such, doctors need to look at a number of variables to diagnose you. This can include a full medical history, a blood test for autoimmune disease and a full physical examination. A full physical examination is necessary as signs and symptoms of autoimmune diseases can show up all over the body. Blood tests will typically include tests for autoantibodies - these are produced when the defect begins to develop - and inflammation or organ function tests. Doctors will run these tests to check if your organs are working correctly, as they are typically affected.

Autoimmune Disease Treatment

There is usually no cure for autoimmune disease, but there is a variety of different autoimmune disease treatment methods for individuals suffering from autoimmune disorder symptoms. The treatment provided will often depend on the severity of the condition in question. However, the goal of treatment is typically not to try and cure the disease, but rather to limit the symptoms and control the process while ensuring that the body can fight back. You might be suffering from a type of autoimmune disease that impacts the level of your thyroid hormone.

Treatment will include a supplement that will provide this missing hormone. Alternatively, issues with the blood can be dealt with using a blood transfusion, while physical therapy may be needed for certain types of the disease. Autoimmune disease Lupus' symptoms include aching and swollen joints, so physical therapy can be highly effective for this condition. Some doctors also believe that diet is a key factor in treating autoimmune diseases and focus treatment plans around this variable. Lectins that are present in gluten and gluten substitutes have been studied potential causes of an autoimmune disorder. It can be useful therefore to try and identify what causes autoimmune disease flare ups for you.

Many people also resort to complementary and alternative medicine (CAM) as a form of treatment for an autoimmune disorder. Examples include acupuncture, chiropractic medicine and natural herbs. However, it's difficult to know how effective these treatments are for conditions like MS and other autoimmune diseases without scientific proof.

The Most Common Autoimmune Diseases

Some of the most common autoimmune disorders are diseases that we hear about every day. People often ask if Rheumatoid Arthritis (RA) and Psoriasis are both autoimmune disorders.

They are, but both can impact on other areas of your body as well. In RA, your immune system begins to attack the cells in your joints by mistake, which leads to symptoms such as swelling, redness and stiffness, whereas Psoriasis causes more skin cells to grow than the body requires, which leads to red and scale-like skin. They share many symptoms such as redness, soreness, and stiffness in the joints. You may also be wondering if Lupus is an autoimmune disorder - it is. The autoimmune disease Lupus will attack a variety of your vital organs, including your heart, and present with some sort of skin irritation.

Because of this, you should not just dismiss any rash you may have. There has been a lot of debate about Multiple Sclerosis (MS) and whether it fits on an autoimmune diseases list. The debate often leaves people wondering if MS is autoimmune or neurological. Due to its complex nature, the cause remains unclear, leaving researchers asking whether MS is an autoimmune disease. This is because MS can present with a variety of neurological symptoms. It is classed as an autoimmune disease because the immune system attacks the protective sheath around nerve cells - the myelin. MS is a problem with your central nervous system and will end up causing a problem with the delivery of messages between your brain and your body. Autoimmune MS symptoms can include issues with walking and coordination. You may also experience numbness in some areas of your body, plus vision, memory, and cognitive problems, although this is by no means an exhaustive list.

Type 1 Diabetes is also classed as an autoimmune disease because it's the result of the immune system mistakenly attacking the cells in the pancreas. It will identify and destroy the insulin cells. This is why people with Type I diabetes need to inject insulin to make sure that the body has enough.

Getting An Autoimmune Disease *NHS Diagnosis*

Autoimmune disease UK patients will generally look for a diagnosis from the NHS. After asking what an autoimmune disease is, and recognising the common symptoms in themselves, people often want to see a professional. A diagnosis on the NHS can be difficult and time consuming, but there are ways to make it easier. First, make sure that you write down a full medical history to give to your doctor. This should include information about family health issues as it could relate to the symptoms. Remember that the autoimmune disorders list is long. A comprehensive list of your symptoms will help your doctor pinpoint the potential condition from which you may be suffering. Make sure that you are keeping a check on your symptoms and try to see a specialist for those that are the most significant.

For instance, an autoimmune kidney disease will likely cause changes in your urination, while an autoimmune skin disease could show as a rash or a severe skin irritation. Be aware that some types of autoimmune disease are easier for doctors to diagnose than others. Being clear on all symptoms can really help. While the autoimmune disorder definition seems simple at first glance, the symptoms, and the impact these diseases can have will vary and can be complex. If you do notice recurring symptoms such as joint pains or swollen glands, it's important to see a doctor. This will help you find out whether you have a condition like rheumatoid arthritis, Addison's disease, or the onset of another autoimmune disease. It's also important to be aware that women are far more likely to develop an autoimmune disorder, while certain diseases are also considered to run in families.

What is Multiple Sclerosis and what are the symptoms?

MS, or Multiple Sclerosis, is a long-term illness that causes many different major and minor symptoms in sufferers. It may impact on your spinal cord, brain, or the eye's optic nerve. MS often causes short and long-term issues with eyesight, balance, walking and muscle control. Lesions can form anywhere on the brain or spinal cord in MS; this means that MS disease symptoms and severity are usually different for each individual. Some people have mild symptoms and do not require therapy (initial symptoms can sometimes be mild and hard to diagnose). Others may have problems performing normal tasks and difficulty with movement or getting around.

MS occurs when your immune system mistakenly attacks myelin, thinking it's a foreign body. Myelin is a fatty sheath-like substance that wraps around your nerve pathways to safeguard them from damage - a little like the insulated coating on an electrical wire. Where this nerve protection is missing or damaged, your nerves can eventually become damaged - this damage presents as white matter lesions in an MRI scan.

When this tissue and nerve damage occurs, your brain cannot send or receive signals through your body properly. The nerve damage can slow down or stop the signals completely, potentially causing issues with movement and feeling in your body, along with the many other symptoms experienced in MS.

The central nervous system connects everything that your body does to the signals to and from your brain. This means that your symptoms are driven by whichever part of your central nervous system is damaged. That is why Multiple Sclerosis and its symptoms often differ from one person to another.

The most common symptoms are: -

- Trouble walking or standing

- Muscle spasms or muscle weakness

- Feeling tired and drained

- Pain or constant aching

- Vision problems, double vision, optic neuritis, focus problems, sometimes only in one eye

- Numbness, lack of feel or tingling "pins and needles" sensations

- Bad bladder or bowel control

- Brain fog, memory, and concentration problems

- Sexual problems

- Depression

The initial symptoms often start between the ages of 20 and 40. However, people are often diagnosed between 40 and 50, and women are three times more likely to be diagnosed with MS. Early symptoms of MS can often be mistaken for other health problems, with many people not seeking a medical diagnosis initially. Potential early signs of multiple sclerosis should not be ignored. Talk to your GP if you have recurring symptoms. Most people with MS suffer regular attacks, known as relapses, during which the illness becomes markedly worse. These are usually followed by instances of recovery when symptoms improve. MS long term behaviour and symptoms are different for each individual. Some people can have long periods of remission but, for many, the disease continues to get worse as time passes. Doctors do not know for certain what causes MS. It is not inherited genetically and passed on to children. Present research suggests that there are over 100 different genes that may impact on your chances of getting MS. As well as family history having very little statistical bearing on MS, ethnic background also has little bearing. There are many things that appear to make getting the disease more likely, and environmental factors may play a role in MS. The further away from the equator you live in your formative years, the higher the statistical chances of getting multiple sclerosis. There is building evidence that shows that having low levels of vitamin D, especially when young, increases the risk of MS. This is linked to an increased rate of MS where there is less sun, as vitamin D is mainly made from exposure to bright sunlight.

Some people may get MS after they have experienced a virus. Studies show that the Epstein-Barr virus or the human herpesvirus 6, which can cause the immune system to stop working normally, can be a factor. These diseases may potentially trigger the illness or trigger MS relapses.

Lifestyle and MS

Smoking and lifestyle choices have also been identified as risk factors that can raise the threat of MS. Research shows that, statistically, you are more likely to get Multiple Sclerosis if you smoke or are exposed to passive smoking. There is also evidence that suggests that stopping smoking can slow down the progression of RRMS to secondary progressive MS. There is also evidence from studies showing that obesity increases the risk that you'll develop MS. This is also related to vitamin D research, as many overweight people have low vitamin D levels. Although there is no direct link between obesity and MS, it is another potential factor that can increase the risk of getting MS. It can be quite difficult initially to diagnose Multiple Sclerosis. The early signs of MS can be very similar to several other autoimmune diseases and some nervous system conditions. If your GP thinks you might potentially have Multiple Sclerosis, then you will usually be referred to a neurologist. As there is no single MS test that specifically identifies the disease, the hospital neurology department will ask you about your general health history. They will then assess you for key indicators of nerve damage in your brain, spinal cord, and optic nerves. The tests to assess and diagnose MS usually comprise:

Neurological and body function tests

These test your balance, vision, strength, reflexes, and coordination, assessing for nerve damage based on your reactions versus normal healthy behaviour.

Blood tests

To rule out or identify diseases that have similar symptoms to MS; e.g. Lyme Disease, vitamin deficiencies, AIDS or neuromyelitis optica.

A lumbar puncture

A test to analyse a sample of the fluid that surrounds the spinal column and brain. The sample will often reveal certain proteins and antibodies (oligoclonal bands) in the spinal fluid. These bands specifically show that the immune system is mistakenly attacking the myelin sheath around the nerves of the central nervous system (the brain and spinal cord).

Evoked potential test

This test measures the electrical activity in the brain, based on how your eyes react to light patterns. This can show if your brain takes longer than normal to receive messages via the nervous system.

Magnetic resonance imaging (MRI) scan

MRI scans use magnetic fields to produce detailed images of your body. They view any damage to the myelin sheath around nerves in the spinal cord and brain. This is often used to confirm a potential Multiple Sclerosis diagnosis.

MS usually begins in one of two ways, either: -

- With symptoms appearing and then disappearing again (relapsing attacks)

- Slow progression of symptoms - sometimes minor - that gradually become worse and worse

There are four primary types of multiple sclerosis (MS):

1. Relapsing-Remitting MS (RRMS): This is the most common type of MS, accounting for approximately 85 percent of cases. People with RRMS experience episodic relapses of symptoms followed by periods of remission, where symptoms may improve or even dissipate completely for a time.

2. Secondary-Progressive MS (SPMS): After some years, many people with RRMS will transition to SPMS, where the disease gradually worsens over time, often with or without intermittent relapses. Most people with MS will eventually develop SPMS.

3. Primary-Progressive MS (PPMS): This is the rarest form of MS, making up

only 5 to 10 percent of cases. People with PPMS experience a gradual worsening of symptoms without any period of remission or improvement. PPMS is often diagnosed later, and is in equal numbers in men and women, unlike RRMS.

4. Progressive-Relapsing MS (PRMS): This type of MS is characterized by a steadily worsening course with occasional relapses and temporary plateaus in symptom severity. PRMS is extremely rare and accounts for around 5 percent of all cases of MS.

There is currently no cure for MS in terms of a treatment that will halt progression and reverse symptoms for everyone with the disease. MS Is a lifelong condition, and individual treatment depends very much on the type of disease and the symptoms of the individual. However, the prognosis for MS patients has improved in recent years, with the advent of HSCT and other new treatments. It should also be noted that long-term studies suggest that MS has only a minor impact on life expectancy.

There are several treatments that have been developed that are shown to help control the disease and the symptoms in some cases. These are: -

- A five-day course of steroids at home to help recovery from relapses

- A similar steroid course of injections administered in hospital

- Specific remedies for individual MS symptoms. These vary widely depending on the prevailing symptoms and would need to be discussed with your GP or neurologist

- Disease modifying drugs (DMDs) or disease modifying therapies (DMTs): these are treatments to slow the progression of MS and reduce the damage to the myelin sheath around the nerves

- Beta interferon injections, to reduce relapses in relapsing remitting MS

- There are several other drugs and therapies licensed by NICE for reducing the impact of MS. The options would need to be discussed with a healthcare professional, your GP or neurologist, before deciding on the best treatment, based on your symptoms and the potential side effects.

The Official NHS Position on Multiple Sclerosis Treatment

The NHS position on the treatment of Multiple Sclerosis is:

"Unfortunately, there is currently no treatment that can slow the progress of primary progressive MS or secondary progressive MS in the absence of relapses. Many therapies aiming to treat progressive MS are currently being researched."

As you may have realised, AIMS is a charity with a focus on HSCT for MS, and the AIMS position is slightly different. The studies and clinical trial results we've seen from those who've had HSCT treatment show that it is very successful at halting the progression of Multiple Sclerosis. There is a very high success rate of over 80% for people with relapsing remitting MS having their progression halted.

HSCT for MS and Autoimmune Disease

What is HSCT for MS?

Even now, HSCT is still something many people have not come across, although it has been around for a lot longer than you might realise. HSCT (also known as BMT, AHSCT or simply ASCT) stands for Haematopoietic Stem Cell Transplant. HSCT should not be confused with 'Stem Cell Therapy' or 'Stem Cell Treatment'. HSCT has been used to treat MS for over 20 years now. Moreover, it was already a well-established treatment, having been performed 2 million times since 1959, when the first ever bone marrow transplant took place. It is currently performed over 50,000 times every year for cancer, and more than 3,000 patients have had HSCT for MS to date, worldwide.

Is HSCT the same as a Bone Marrow Transplant (BMT)?

Stem cell transplants and bone marrow transplants seem to get mixed up - but are they the same thing? Essentially, yes; in HSCT for MS the stem cells must come from the bone marrow and in this context a bone marrow transplant is synonymous with HSCT, Haematopoietic Stem Cell Transplant, Autologous Stem Cell Transplant or Autologous Haematopoietic Stem Cell Transplant.

What is the process of a Stem Cell Transplant?

HSCT is a procedure that works by ablating (wiping out) the faulty T and B lymphocyte cells that work to damage the immune system in MS and other haematologically rooted autoimmune conditions. This ablation is achieved with chemotherapy; it is important to note that stem cells alone will not achieve the desired result. When the faulty immune system and the T and B lymphocytes have been wiped out with chemotherapy, naïve stem cells are re-infused into the body. These cells have no memory of MS and are harvested from the patient prior to the wiping out of the immune system with chemotherapy. The stem cells work to help rebuild a new, functional immune system for the patient - one that is no longer attacking itself. The aim of HSCT is to halt progression, but many patients see symptomatic improvements too.

What is the difference between Myeloablative and Non- Myeloablative HSCT?

The difference between Myeloablative and Non-Myeloablative HSCT can sometimes confuse people. All HSCT protocols for the treatment of autoimmune disorders, and MS specifically, ablate the T and B cells in the body that are responsible for the underlying nerve damage/ destruction. However, HSCT protocols run a spectrum from complete in-vivo lymphocyte ablation (the myeloablative protocols) to partial in-vivo myeloablation (non-myeloablative protocols, also sometimes referred to as "Reduced Intensity Conditioning" (RIC) regimens). There has been no head-to-head comparison of the two approaches.

What is the difference between an Autologous and an Allogeneic Transplant?

Patients are sometimes confused by the difference between allogeneic and autologous HSCT. Allogeneic simply means that the cells are harvested from a donor; autologous means they come from your own body.

What is Engraftment?

Engraftment is when the new cells find their way to the bone marrow and can then begin the process of making new, healthy cells. This process can take between 10 days and a month, and during this time the patient has no effective immune system and must therefore be extra cautious when it comes to avoiding infection.

How much does HSCT cost?

In the UK, HSCT can be received on the NHS if the patient meets certain criteria. However, different funding rules in England, Scotland, Wales, and NI can mean that acceptance success can be variable. Notwithstanding the funding conditions in different areas, patients must also get a referral to a neurologist from the London MDT via their GP/neurologist (England) or neurologist (rest of the UK). The criteria are detailed on the AIMS website. HSCT is also offered in Sheffield under slightly different criteria.

HSCT is available privately in the UK from around £90,000. Internationally, the cost of HSCT can vary. The two international hospitals that AIMS supports are the Clinica Ruiz hospitals in Puebla and Monterey, Mexico, and AA Maximov hospital in Moscow, Russia. At the time of writing, HSCT is currently available (for accepted patients) for 47,000 Euros in Moscow (around £41,500 at current exchange rates) or 57,500 USO in Mexico (around £48k at current exchange rates, not including travel expenses).

How long does it take to recover from HSCT?

People are often concerned about the time it takes to recover from HSCT, and recovery times can vary, but the patient is usually well enough to leave the hospital within two or three weeks of the transplant. On discharge from hospital, many patients choose to follow a neutropenic diet for up to six months, and various precautions should be taken in terms of hygiene and avoiding infection - the most important of these being frequent handwashing. AIMS has known people return to work in as little as 2-3 months, but recovery will be different for everyone.

What are the mortality risks of HSCT?

At AIMS, we feel it is important to discuss the mortality risks involved with HSCT. As with any medical procedure, there is an element of risk, and HSCT involves chemotherapy which does carry its own risks. However, before being accepted for HSCT, the patient will have many thorough medical checks to ensure that the treatment is suitable for them - this is the case at all HSCT hospitals AIMS supports. HSCT has a very small mortality risk. However that risk varies significantly depending on the type of HSCT used. The non-myeloablative HSCT which is used in the UK and by the international hospitals supported by AIMS has a global mortality risk of approximately 0.3%. Myeloablative HSCT, which completely ablates the immune system, isn't used as often these days, and has a higher rate of mortality.

AIMS Charity - A Bit About Us:

In 2011, my husband, James Coates, was diagnosed with Multiple Sclerosis. What began as an annoying sensation in his leg (foot drop), rapidly progressed to a whole host of limiting symptoms. Over the course of the next 5 years, James tried several different things to slow down or halt his progression. As a person with Secondary Progressive Multiple Sclerosis, he had a limited number of options.

In 2014, we came across something called a Haematopoietic Stem Cell Transplant. On querying the treatment with neurologists, we received two reactions - the first "Can you spell that for me? I'll look into it," and the second "I'm afraid I'd only recommend HSCT to someone with six months to live - it's extremely dangerous and experimental." This was to be an introduction to the general misinformation offered by (some) neurologists in respect of HSCT, and it has become a recurring theme as we at AIMS know, having spoken to many hundreds of MS patients on the journey to halt their progression.

We were not deterred, and continued to research HSCT which, far from being an experimental treatment for MS, has been performed for the condition for over 20 years now. As previously mentioned, Autologous HSCT for MS has a mortality rate of around 0.3% (according to Dr Richard K Burt, pioneer of HSCT for MS, speaking at the 2016 International HSCT Symposium in Sheffield). To put this into context, a 2006 study from the Royal Marsden Hospital ("Mortality within 30 days of Chemotherapy: a clinical governance benchmarking issue for oncology patients":

MER O'Brien, A Borthwick and IE Smith - published by Cancer Research UK) found that there was a mortality rate of 1.5% in patients who were receiving potentially curative chemotherapy for gastrointestinal malignancy - that is, five times the mortality rate of HSCT for MS.

James was fortunate enough to be referred to King's College Hospital, London, and was accepted for transplant in January 2016 - right before the BBC TV Panorama episode 'Can You Stop My MS?' aired. Immediately after this, more and more patients asked their doctors for referrals for this supposed 'miracle cure'. Many of the neurologists simply didn't know how to respond, as HSCT is often out of their field of experience. Others seemed annoyed at having their professional opinion challenged and refused to refer. Many, many patients - a lot of them with a stronger case for acceptance than James believed that he had ever had - were being turned away on the basis that their neurologist said they would not meet the criteria. We began to see a huge influx of members in the UK HSCT forums, as people desperately searched for answers and support. We found that a lot of misinformation was being given to MS patients ("HSCT will kill you", "HSCT doesn't work on your type of MS", "HSCT can only be used if you're under 40" and many variations on the same theme). It became clear that of the estimated 130,000 people in the UK with MS, most of them were not being given accurate information about HSCT - and at the time of publication of this book, this is still the case.

James had a successful transplant on July 25th, 2016. Over the following weeks and months, he discovered that he was seeing improvement in many of his other symptoms. James' mobility remains the same, as the damage causing his foot drop was permanent in SPMS, but his overall quality of life improved enormously - this is still the case. As he began his recovery, James and I felt very strongly that we wanted to help others on this same journey to halt their MS. It quickly became apparent that there were other like-minded individuals who felt the same way- and thus AIMS was born.

Our trustees have either had HSCT themselves or they have MS (like James, Becky, our former trustee Ann, Janet, Laura, Preeti, Damien, former trustee Philippa, and Adrian), or they are the partner of someone who has had HSCT (Alison). All of them are fully committed to supporting people seeking HSCT for MS.

AIMS Mission Statement

To preserve and protect the health and well-being of UK patients suffering from Multiple Sclerosis and Autoimmune disease, in the provision of signposting, support and grants.

What Does AIMS Do?

We provide support to MS and Autoimmune patients through telephone calls, zoom meetings, emails, and social media groups, and by advocating with and for patients. We present to stakeholders, and we lobby for change. AIMS works with charities such as the MS-TRUST, The MS Society and MS UK, as well as with global specialists in the provision of HSCT. AIMS does not receive any funding from pharmaceutical companies or from stakeholders; we are non-partisan and independent. Our funding generally comes from donations from people on the MS journey. As well as support, advocacy, awareness-raising and lobbying, AIMS also provides travel grants for UK residents who are undergoing HSCT for MS. Our website www.aimscharity.org provides an opportunity for patients to book a 1-2-1 call with one of our trained peer support consultants, the form to apply for a travel grant, a 'myth busting' section, videos of interviews with the world's leading HSCT specialists, fundraising hints and tips, and collated peer-reviewed research into HSCT.

AIMS is currently supporting the StarMS trials which are underway in the UK.

StarMS is comparing HSCT against high efficacy drugs for MS, to determine the best treatment for highly active RRMS. You can read more about StarMS on our website, and here:

https://www.sheffield.ac.uk/scharr/research/centres/ctru/starms

If you would like to support AIMS, you can make a purchase from our shop or make a donation to us using a variety of payment options:

https://www.aimscharity.org/donate

The Neutropenic Diet: The Basics

What is neutropenia?

Neutrophils are white blood cells - they help to destroy bacteria. If your neutrophil count is low, then you are at more risk of infection than people whose neutrophil levels are within the normal range.

Why should I still follow this diet even if I'm no longer neutropenic?

If you have had HSCT, your neutrophil levels will probably have risen while you were still in hospital, and by the time you left hospital you were probably no longer neutropenic. However, your neutrophil levels will still be relatively low and can fluctuate for many months following transplant. For this reason, it is prudent to follow a low-risk diet post- transplant.

How low risk does it need to be?

There's no question that there is much controversy surrounding the neutropenic diet. The rationale behind not eating raw fruit and veg is that there are bacteria in salads; bacteria cause infections, so immunocompromised patients are at increased risk for infections, and therefore - no salad. However, there's also an argument that restricting fruits and vegetables may even increase the risk of infection and compromise the immune-compromised patient's nutritional status. There have been numerous randomised studies done to test the value of an all-cooked vs raw food diet for the immunocompromised, and some research suggests that there is actually no difference in infection and death rates between the two diets. But that is not to say that there is not a real and substantial risk for the immunocompromised patient from food poisoning caused by infections such as Salmonella Norovirus, Campylobacter, E. coli, Listeria and Clostridium perfringens. The Haematology Group of the British Dietetic

Association's established recommendations were published by Leukaemia and Lymphoma Research in 2007, but the evidence for this guidance was subsequently re-visited. The recipes in this book follow the revised guidance from the BOA, published in May 2016, which suggests that the immunocompromised patient should avoid all unnecessary risk of potentially life-threatening infections.

What are the ten basic principles of a neutropenic diet?

1. Avoid all fresh fruit and vegetables and frozen fruit. Avoid fresh garnishes such as salads and herbs
2. Cooked vegetables, tinned produce and pasteurised juices are fine
3. Avoid salad bars, fruit bars, delis, fresh baked goods, and food markets
4. Avoid eating or drinking in restaurants or on aeroplanes etc...
5. Avoid rare or undercooked meat and fish
6. Avoid raw nuts and seeds - baked products with these ingredients are fine
7. Make sure all dairy products are pasteurised
8. Avoid yoghurt labelled 'bio' or 'probiotic' - live yoghurt is safe to use
9. Avoid lightly cooked eggs or products containing raw egg
10. Practise good food hygiene. Ensure that you always wash your hands before and after handling food, ensure all utensils are clean, separate raw food from cooked food, and keep hot food hot and cold food cold

Neutropenic FAQ

Find Many More Q&A at

https:/ltinyurl.com/ TheNeutropenicKitchen

Can I eat Quorn on a neutropenic diet?
Quorn is perfectly safe to eat on this diet.

What about prawns / shellfish?
If thoroughly cooked, shellfish should be safe for you to eat as it is a food which is carefully monitored in the production process. However, shellfish is still a food that has been known to cause food poisoning - even at world class restaurants - so approach with caution.

Can I use frozen fruit/ berries on this diet?
No - they're best avoided as certain strains of bacteria can survive the freezing/thawing process.

Should I drink bottled water instead of tap water?
Funnily enough, tap water (in countries where it is safe to drink the tap water ordinarily) is considered safer than bottled water. Bottled water is not sterile and should be avoided. Similarly, bought ice cubes should also be avoided. It has been suggested that running the tap for a couple of minutes reduces the risk of infection. Well water is acceptable if boiled for at least 1 minute.
However, if you really want to use bottled water, then ensure it is marked:

Reverse osmosis or
Distillation or
Filter of an absolute 1 micron or smaller.

Are seeds safe to eat?

If cooked/ toasted, yes; if raw, no.

Is it safe for me to reheat food?

If you cool the food quickly, store it at under 5 degrees in a fridge for no more than 24 hours, and reheat until piping hot and for the most part you should be ok. The BOA found there was no evidence to suggest that correctly reheated food increases food poisoning risk in immunocompromised individuals. The exception to this is the reheating of cooked rice. The spores of Bacillus cereus and Bacillus subtilis, found in rice, survive the cooking process.

These develop into bacteria that multiply very quickly at ambient temperatures and may not be adequately killed during reheating. Therefore, rice should be served hot and eaten immediately after it is first cooked.

Can I use a slow cooker, or will it not be hot enough?

A slow cooker is an excellent piece of kit to own and will cook your food thoroughly and safely. Your coffee maker, however, probably won't get hot enough as it won't reach boiling point.

Can I use herbs and spices?

Yes, but you must ensure that they are thoroughly cooked, so the heat kills any potential spores or bacteria. Dried herbs are fine to use in cooking too.

Can I sprinkle black pepper on my food to season it after cooking? No - avoid this. Black pepper can carry a particular fungus, and so it needs to be cooked if used. You may add salt without any problem.

Can I use soft cheeses like Philadelphia?
Yes, pasteurised, processed, commercially packaged cheeses such as those found in supermarkets are fine. However, avoid unpasteurised, soft cheeses such as Camembert and Brie (read the label - it will tell you if it's unpasteurised), and any blue cheese or cheese with a mould.

Can I still eat bread?
Yes, but avoid bakery fresh bread and stick to homemade or pre-packaged.

Can I have yoghurt?
You can. However, avoid bio yoghurts or anything labelled probiotic as the 'good bacteria' is no good for a weakened immune system! Live yoghurt, however, is fine.

Can I go out for tea / coffee?
This is best avoided for the first few months, as well as drinking hot beverages made on trains or planes - you can't be sure of the hygiene practices and, as mentioned above, the water probably won't be boiling.

Can I dine out/ get a takeaway?
This is best avoided for the first six months, and even then, should be approached with caution - ensure the restaurant has a high hygiene rating, and continue to avoid things like rare meat, certain soft cheeses and so on.

Hopefully, the recipes in this book will inspire you enough to ensure that you don't feel you're missing out in the first few months - there are several 'takeaway' recipes. I hope that you enjoy them as much as we do.

Can I use the BBQ?
Of the millions of cases of food poisoning every year, a high proportion are caused by BBQ food, and the food poisoning rates shoot up in the summer months. Personally, I'd avoid the BBQ for the first summer after HSCT, but if you must use it, ensure that the coals are glowing red with a layer of ash. Move the food around regularly to ensure even cooking, and ensure the food is cooked thoroughly and is not pink. Serve it straight away or keep it in a hot oven. Take great care not to cross contaminate raw and cooked meat.

Is chorizo OK to eat?
Chorizo used as an ingredient in cooked dishes is fine, but avoid using cooked, chilled chorizo.

What about pate?
Pasteurised pate and paste in tins or jars that do not need to be refrigerated BEFORE OPENING are fine.

My dried herbs / spices are out of date - are they still OK to use? Within reason, they should be fine although the flavour may deteriorate over time. They shouldn't do you any harm if they're thoroughly cooked.

For how long should I follow this diet if I've had HSCT?
It's very much a personal choice, and while it may be safe for you to relax the requirements, and even dine out again, after a period of time has passed, it is still important to avoid certain foods for at least six months.

Your medical practitioner will be able to offer you further guidance. The neutropenic diet isn't compulsory - it's all about risk assessment and risk management.

The Neutropenic Diet

Meat & Fish

Recommended	Avoid
• Tinned tuna or other fish • Tinned meat • Any piping hot cooked meat or fish • Frozen meat or fish cooked well and served hot • Vacuum-packed cold meats such as turkey and ham stored below 3°C and eaten according to the manufacturer's instructions • Smoked salmon from a freshly opened vacuum pack • Pasteurised pâté and paste in tins or jars that do not need to be refrigerated before opening	• Raw, rare or cold meat including cold sausage or salami, or cold cuts from a deli counter • Canned meats that have been opened and stored • Raw / undercooked poultry, meat or fish • Sushi • Caviar • Oysters • Cold smoked or pickled meat or fish • Sashimi • Fast food • Fresh, refrigerated pâté

The Neutropenic Diet

Dairy

Recommended	Avoid
<ul><li>Hard cooked eggs; scrambled, omelette, hard boiled</li><li>Pasteurised milk, cream, butter and cheeses</li><li>Any yoghurt that does not describe itself as bio or probiotic (including live, plain, Greek and fruit yoghurts)</li><li>Commercially produced mayonnaise</li><li>Non-dairy creamers</li><li>Sour cream, crème fraîche</li><li>Commercial eggnog</li><li>Commercial custard</li><li>Commercial milkshakes</li><li>Aerosol cream</li><li>Commercially packed parmesan</li><li>Commercially packaged cream cheese such as Philadelphia</li><li>Processed cheeses and cheese singles</li><li>Non-mouldy cheeses</li><li>Canned or powdered supplement drinks</li><li>Pasteurised egg substitutes</li></ul>	<ul><li>Soft boiled eggs or runny fried eggs</li><li>Anything made with raw eggs such as hollandaise, béarnaise, mayonnaise, home made Caesar salad dressing, home made custard based desserts etc...</li><li>Cheeses with mould such as Gorgonzola, Roquefort, Stilton</li><li>Soft cheeses such as Brie, Camembert, Feta</li><li>Ice cream made with raw egg</li><li>Cheeses with uncooked vegetables</li><li>Mexican style cheeses</li><li>Eggnog made with raw egg</li><li>Bio or probiotic yoghurt such as Yakult or Actimel</li></ul>

The Neutropenic Diet

Vegetables, Herbs & Spices

Recommended	Avoid
• Frozen or tinned veg including beans and legumes • Dry or fresh herbs added during the cooking process • Tinned / carton vegetable juices and soups • Frozen meat or fish cooked well and served hot • Pickles in jars or cans • Fresh vegetables cooked thoroughly (the heating process kills the bacteria)	• Fresh, raw vegetables and salads including stuffed vine leaves, fattoush and tabouleh • Fresh herbs or spices added after cooking • Black pepper added after cooking • Any miso products • Apple Cider Vinegar (with the mother) • Stir fried vegetables • Fresh Sauerkraut • Home made pickles and fermented products

The Neutropenic Diet

Grains, Cereals & Bread

Recommended

- Any pre-packaged, shop-bought bread
- Any packaged snacks such as crisps, pretzels, popcorn, tortilla chips etc...
- Cooked, hot pasta and rice, couscous, quinoa etc...
- Cooked grains such as oatmeal and wheat
- Instant hot cereal such as Ready Brek etc...
- Home made bread
- Cooked and processed dried fruit such as flapjacks, most cereal bars (check them), fruit cakes and scones

Avoid

- Raw grains
- Fresh baked goods from a bakery
- Uncooked grain products
- Cold pasta and rice
- Reheated rice
- Bread with raw nuts or seeds
- Cereals with raw nuts or seeds
- Products containing raw, dried fruit such as muesli or Bombay mix

The Neutropenic Diet

Fruit & Nuts

Recommended	Avoid
<ul><li>Any tinned fruit</li><li>Cooked fruit</li><li>Concentrated or pasteurised fruit juice</li><li>Roasted / cooked nuts and seeds</li><li>Commercial nut butters</li></ul>	<ul><li>Frozen fruit that isn't going to be cooked</li><li>Raw nuts and seeds</li><li>Nuts in their shells</li><li>Freshly squeezed juices</li><li>Fresh fruit unless it has a very thick skin like a pineapple.</li></ul>

The Neutropenic Diet

Desserts / Sweets

Recommended	Avoid
• Refrigerated commercial desserts, puddings and cakes • Jelly • Baked cookies • Commercial ice creams and ice lollies • Pasteurised ice cream made without egg • Syrups • Jam	• Any dessert that should have been kept in the fridge but hasn't been • Bakery desserts • Ice cream made with raw egg or unpasteurised products • Previously thawed and re-frozen ice cream • Soft serve ice cream from a machine such as Mr Whippy • Honey

The Neutropenic Diet

Drinks

Recommended	Avoid
• Tap water • Distilled bottled water • Canned drinks • Pasteurised milk • Hot tea or coffee made with boiling water • Pasteurised juices • Cordials • Ice made from tap water	• Bottled water that is not distilled • Cold brewed tea or coffee • Water from fresh wells • Unpasteurised juices • Commercially bought ice

The RECIPES

UNLESS OTHERWISE STATED,

RECIPES INCLUDE QUANTITIES TO MAKE 4 PORTIONS

BONUS RECIPE

CHICKEN KYIV PP60-61

POULTRY

BUTTER CHICKEN PP62-63

CAJUN CHICKEN PP64-65

CHEATS' DUCK A L'ORANGE PP66-67

CHEATS' PAELLA PP68-69

CHICKEN AND CASHEW NUTS PP70-71

CHICKEN AND MUSHROOM PAPPARDELLE P72

CHICKEN AND TARRAGON BAKE PP72-73

CHICKEN AND TARRAGON PIE PP74-75

CHICKEN ENCHILADAS P76

CHICKEN KORMA PP76-77

CHICKEN MILANESE WITH NEAPOLITAN SPAGHETTI P77

CHICKEN MOLE AKA CHILLI CHOCOLATE CHICKEN PP78-79

CHICKEN SATAY SKEWERS WITH PEANUT DIPPING SAUCE PP80-81

CHICKEN PAPPARDELLE WITH CREAMY PESTO SAUCE P82

CHILLI CHICKEN NACHOS PP83-84

CREAMY GARLIC CHICKEN AND MUSHROOMS P85

CREAMY CHICKEN AND TOMATO GNOCCHI WITH SPINACH PP85-86

CREAMY CHICKEN CREPES PP87-88

CRUNCHY COCONUT CHICKEN P89

CRUNCHY JERK CHICKEN P90

DILL AND CORIANDER CHICKEN WITH BROCCOLI, ONION, AND SPINACH PASTA PP90-91

FAKEAWAY SPICY CRUNCHY CHICKEN PP91-92

FUSION CHICKEN P93

HUNTER'S CHICKEN PP94-95

LEMON CHICKEN PP96-97

MOZZARELLA-STUFFED PANCETTA-WRAPPED CHICKEN PP98-99

PAN-FRIED DUCK BREAST WITH BLACKBERRY JUS PP100-101

ROAST POUSSIN P102

SALT AND PEPPER CHICKEN PP102-103

SPINACH, GARLIC, & HERB CHICKEN P103

STICKY CHINESE CHICKEN PP104-105

STICKY SALTED CARAMEL CHICKEN P106

STICKY SESAME CHICKEN PP106-107

SWEET CHILLI GARLIC AND GINGER CHICKEN P108

TANDOORI CHICKEN KEBABS PP108-109

THAI GREEN CHICKEN CURRY PP110-111

THYME AND JUNIPER DUCK WITH MUSHROOM RISOTTO PP112-113

MEAT

BEEF STEW AND DUMPLINGS PP114-115

BEEF WITH GREEN PEPPER AND BLACK BEAN SAUCE PP116-117

BRAISED BEEF TAGLIATELLE PP118-119

CHEATS' CARBONARA PP120-121

CHEESEBURGER PP122-123

CHILLI PP124-125

CORNED BEEF MASH P126

DAVID AND PAOLA'S SPAGHETTI BOLOGNESE PP126-127

GOULASH PP128-129

LAMB IN RED WINE, GARLIC, THYME, AND ROSEMARY GRAVY PP130-131

LAMB TIKKA PP132-133

LANCASHIRE HOTPOT PP134-135

MOUSSAKA PP136-137

PORK LOIN IN CIDER, SAGE, AND WHOLEGRAIN MUSTARD SAUCE PP138-139

PORK LOIN IN SAGE, ONION, AND APPLE SAUCE PP140-141

POSH LASAGNE PP142-143

SAUSAGE AND BEAN CASSEROLE P144

SHEPHERD'S PIE PP144-145

SLOW COOKED PULLED PORK PP146-147

SLOW COOKED STEAK WITH MUSHROOM AND THYME SAUCE PP148-149

SPAGHETTI AND MEATBALLS PP150-151

SPECIAL FRIED RICE PP152-153

STEAK PARMIGIANA PP154-155

TERIYAKI STEAK PP156-157

TOAD IN THE HOLE PP158-159

VILLETTA PIE PP160-161

FISH

COD MORNAY PP162-163

COD IN PARSLEY SAUCE PP164-165

COCONUT SALMON CURRY PP166-167

CUMIN AND CORIANDER CRUSTED SALMON P168

FABULOUS FISH PIES PP168-170

FILO-TOPPED FISH PIE PP171-172

HERB AND CAPER SEA BASS P173

HERBY FISH BAKE PP174-175

KING PRAWN, BUTTERNUT SQUASH, BACON, SPINACH AND GARLIC PASTA P174

LEMON AND MAPLE BAKED SALMON WITH MINTED PEA AND ASPARAGUS RISOTTO PP176-177

LEMON LINGUINE WITH SMOKED SALMON AND CHIVES PP178-179

MUM'S CHEESY FISH CRUMBLE P180

ORANGE AND HERB CRUSTED SALMON P180

PAN FRIED SALMON WITH KING PRAWN, SMOKED SALMON, AND WATERCRESS SAUCE P181

PESTO CRUSTED SALMON P181

PRAWN, FENNEL, AND SPINACH PASTA PP182-183

SALMON CROQUE MONSIEUR PP184-185

SALMON WITH TOMATO CHAMPAGNE AND CRAB MEAT RISOTTO PP186-187

SEAFOOD CHOWDER PP188-189

SMOKED HADDOCK FLORENTINE P190

SPICED COD PP190-191

TERIYAKI SALMON P192

TUNA PASTA BAKE PP192-193

VEGETARIAN

ASPARAGUS AND PINE NUT PASTA P194

CHEATS' FONDUE PP195-196

CHEATS' PIZZA P195

CHEESE AND BROCCOLI PASTA P197

CHEESE X4 AND CHIVE RISOTTO PP197-198

CREAMY SPINACH AND TOMATO GNOCCHI PP198-199

MAC 'N' CHEESE PP200-201

MEDITERRANEAN PASTA PP201-203

MUSHROOM RISOTTO PP204-205

MUSHROOM, SAGE, AND PECAN RAVIOLI PP206-207

PAULINE'S CHICKPEA CURRY PP208-209

RED ONION MARMALADE AND GOAT'S CHEESE TART PP210-211

SPINACH AND RICOTTA LASAGNE PP212-213

VEGETABLE LASAGNE PP214-215

CHICKEN KYIV

Chicken Kyiv (CAN BE GLUTEN FREE)

As I'm writing this, the Ukraine war has been going on for exactly a year, so I'm adding this recipe as a special extra at the start of this book. Our hearts go out to all involved in this terrible conflict, as well as our Russian friends at AA Maximov Hospital for HSCT in Moscow. The recipe is spelt 'Kyiv' as a mark of respect, rather than the 'Kiev' that we're probably all used to. For me, this dish will be 'Chicken Kyiv' from now on. Home-made chicken Kyiv is so much nicer than anything you will buy in the shops, and it's really not that hard to make.
Serve this with simple steamed veggies and potatoes - my kids love triple cooked chips with this!

Ingredients:
4 large chicken breasts
4 slices of white bread (use gluten free bread if preferred - it works equally well)
2 tsp chopped garlic/ garlic paste
1 tbsp finely chopped parsley (dried is fine too)
100g salted butter (or dairy free spread if preferred - Vitalite works very well)
2 eggs, whisked and placed in a bowl
cornflour for coating
1/2 tsp smoked paprika
salt and pepper
2 tbsp vegetable oil

Preheat oven to 180°C. Let the butter soften a little, before adding the parsley and garlic and mixing thoroughly. Using a sharp knife, find the thickest side of the chicken breast and make a deep pocket in that side. Divide the butter mix into four, and poke it into each pocket, getting it in as deeply as possible - a piping bag is ideal for this if you have one to hand. Finely chop the bread into breadcrumbs using a food processor or blender. Place the breadcrumbs in a bowl and season with the salt, pepper and smoked paprika. Now dip the stuffed chicken breasts firstly into the cornflour, then the egg and finally the breadcrumbs. Repeat this process so they have a double coating as this will help to prevent the butter oozing out during cooking. Fry the Kyivs in the oil for 2-3 minutes each side, until golden brown, then transfer to a baking tray. Bake for 25-30 minutes or until cooked through.

Poultry

BUTTER CHICKEN

Butter Chicken (GLUTEN FREE)
This is absolutely my favourite slow cooker recipe ever, so it seems a fitting one to start with! Difficulty: 7/10

Our testers said 'Fan-bloomin'-tastic!'

Ingredients:
2 onions - roughly chopped
3 garlic cloves
4cm fresh root ginger
8 boneless, skinless chicken thighs
1 tbsp sunflower oil
25g butter
1 tsp crushed cumin seeds
1 tsp crushed fennel seeds
4 crushed cardamom pods
1 tsp paprika
1 tsp ground turmeric
1/4 tsp ground cinnamon
300 ml chicken stock
100 ml double cream
1 tbsp brown sugar
2 tbsp tomato puree pinch of salt
toasted flaked almonds to garnish

Blend onions, garlic, and ginger in a blender. Cut the chicken into large chunks, and brown in the sunflower oil in a frying pan. Transfer to a plate. Add the butter to the pan, then the onion paste. Cook slowly until it begins to colour. Stir in the crushed and ground spices and cook for 1 minute. Mix in the stock, sugar, tomato purée and salt, and bring to the boil. Transfer the chicken and the sauce to a slow cooker and cook on low for 6-6 1/2 hours. Stir in the cream and cover and cook for a further 15 minutes. Garnish with toasted, flaked almonds and serve with rice.

CAJUN CHICKEN

Cajun Chicken (GLUTEN FREE)
Possibly the unanimous family favourite of my recipes - both James and our girls love this one, because it's so tasty. There's a little bit of prep involved, but it's worth it!
Difficulty 5/10

Our testers said: "For me everything was achievable without any problems. Instead of the sweetcorn I opted for garlic mushrooms with spinach. Beautiful!"

Ingredients:
4 boneless chicken breasts or 8 chicken thighs, if preferred
4 large potatoes - washed but unpeeled
2 tsp Cajun seasoning plus more for the wedges (I use Barts blend, which comes in a tin - it's not overly hot, which appeals to me)
1 tsp smoked paprika
4 cobs of sweetcorn
mini wooden corn skewers (soaked in water for 1 hour)
Maldon sea salt
100ml olive oil & more for drizzling

Preheat the oven to 180°C. Cut the four potatoes into wedges, place on the largest baking tray you have, drizzle with olive oil and Cajun seasoning Just a couple of teaspoons), leaving space for the sweetcorn. Mix 2 teaspoons of Cajun seasoning with 1 teaspoon of smoked paprika and 100ml of olive oil in a large bowl. Coat the chicken thoroughly with the mixture and place the chicken breasts on another baking tray. Cut the sweetcorn in half and insert a mini skewer into each one. Add the 8 halved pieces of sweetcorn to the tray with the potatoes.
Place the chicken on the middle shelf of the oven, and the potatoes and corn on the top. Turn the corn, potatoes, and chicken after 20 minutes and continue cooking for a further 20 minutes. Turn again and continue to cook until the potatoes are golden brown, and the sweetcorn is starting to blacken at the edges. The chicken will make its own thin sauce, which you can spoon over the top. Sprinkle some Maldon sea salt over the potato wedges for the final touch, and I love to slather the sweetcorn with some butter!

Cheats' Duck a l'Orange with Crispy Potatoes and Root Vegetables (GLUTEN FREE)
A lovely one for a dinner party, or maybe as a treat for Xmas / New Year. The orange sauce is delicious and deceptively simple. Difficulty: 5/10

Ingredients:
4 duck quarters (skin on)
chopped root vegetables to taste (carrot, turnip, parsnip, and red onion)
seasoning
vegetable oil for roasting the vegetables
200g charlotte potatoes, finely sliced
2 tbsp of Cointreau (or other orange liqueur such as Grand Marnier or triple sec)
2 tbsp of marmalade without peel
zest and juice of 1 orange
handful of chopped thyme
2 tbsp maple syrup (honey works as well but not for a neutropenic diet)

Preheat oven to 200°C. Roast the root vegetables for 30-40 minutes or until caramelised. Reduce the temperature to 170°C and remove the vegetables and keep them warm. Place the Cointreau, marmalade, orange juice and zest, thyme and maple syrup in a saucepan and reduce a little until you have a sticky sauce. Place the duck on a trivet over a roasting pan in the oven for about 90 minutes on 170°C, or until the skin is golden and crispy. When the duck is cooked, simply pour the sauce over the top. Really very easy, but a bit of a show stopper. Sauté the potatoes in a little oil and season with fine sea salt. Serve with the sauté potatoes and the roasted root vegetables.

CHEATS' DUCK A L'ORANGE

Cheats' Paella (GLUTEN FREE)
This is a nice, quick alternative to traditionally cooked paella - if I can make something tasty that's going to take me a fraction of the time and effort, I'm always going to do that. There are never any leftovers with this one and it's always requested when our daughters are visiting. Buy ready chopped veg to make this one even easier. Difficulty: 3/10

Ingredients
8 boneless chicken thighs
200g chopped cooking chorizo
200g raw king prawns
red, yellow & orange pepper - chopped (1 of each)
1.5L chicken stock
1 red onion - chopped
1 bulb garlic (peeled, but with the cloves left whole)
2 tbsp olive oil
2 tsp smoked paprika
300g paella rice
salt and black pepper (when cooking)

Preheat oven to 180°C. Roast boneless chicken thighs, chopped chorizo, chopped red, yellow, and orange peppers, garlic and chopped red onion in olive oil and 2 teaspoons of smoked paprika, salt & pepper (a bit of Jack Daniels BBQ marinade is nice with this too, or a capful of Stubbs Liquid Smoke) at 180°C. After about half an hour, when it's all caramelised and lovely, tip in the paella rice and cover the whole lot with chicken stock (a good 1.5 litres of it).

Cook for another 30 minutes, then add raw prawns (I usually marinate them in garlic, olive oil and lemon juice and zest first) for a further 10 minutes until they are pink and thoroughly cooked through. Season to taste (avoid raw black pepper and fresh herbs on the top though).

CHEATS' PAELLA

CHICKEN AND CASHEW NUTS

Chicken and Cashew Nuts (GLUTEN FREE)
Broccoli florets go particularly well with this dish. Wash then steam them (an excellent way to kill bacteria) and add them to the dish just before serving. This is a staple in our house. Make it even easier by serving it with microwaved rice.
Difficulty: 4/10

Ingredients:
1 tbsp sesame oil
4 chicken breasts - cubed
5cm chunk of fresh ginger - minced
200g salted cashew nuts
1 tbsp minced garlic
(or to taste - we do like our garlic!)
1/2 tbsp dark soy sauce
1 tbsp cornflour
400ml chicken stock
1 head of broccoli divided into florets

Gently fry the chicken in the sesame oil until it browns. Add the ginger, garlic, and cashew nuts, and broccoli and cook for another 5-6 minutes, until the cashew nuts start to colour. Add the cornflour and mix until it's absorbed (it will look pretty gooey and disgusting at this stage - don't worry, it's fine). Add the stock and the soy sauce and bring to the boil. Simmer on a low heat until the sauce is thick and glossy - you can add a little more water to thin the sauce if it gets too thick. Serve with rice or noodles.

Chicken and Mushroom Pappardelle (CAN BE GLUTEN FREE)
An easy, mid-week kind of dinner. Substitute with gluten free pasta if required. Use tofu if vegetarian. Difficulty 3/10

Ingredients:
dried Pappardelle ribbons (400g)
8 boneless chicken thighs cut into cubes
1tbsp olive oil
200ml double cream/ Elmlea double (dairy or plant)
200ml chicken / vegetable stock
320g sliced mushrooms
handful of chopped tarragon

Boil the pasta in chicken stock until cooked. While the pasta is cooking, fry the mushrooms and chicken in the olive oil until golden brown. Add the handful of chopped tarragon and stir until wilted. Transfer the chicken and mushroom mixture into the pasta and add the stock and cream. Stir and reduce until the sauce coats the pasta.

Chicken and Tarragon Bake (GLUTEN FREE)
*It's really a chicken tarragon and **parsley** bake, but the tarragon is the dominant flavour in this one. I use fresh herbs but dried is fine too. Difficulty 3/10*

Our testers said: "This dish had something familiar and homely about it, although I had never eaten it before. Large mushroom caps could work instead of the chicken for vegetarians, plus veg stock for the sauce."

Ingredients:
4 chicken breasts
1 onion, finely chopped
1 tbsp butter
1 tbsp cornflour
1/2 tsp onion powder
1/2 tsp garlic powder
1/2 tsp mustard powder
1 tsp white wine vinegar
1 heaped tbsp tarragon
1 heaped tbsp parsley
salt and pepper

250 ml milk
250 ml chicken stock
50g finely grated Parmesan

Preheat oven to 180°C. Brown the chicken in a little oil and set aside in an oven proof dish. In the same pan, melt the butter and add the onions to soften. When the onions are cooked, add the garlic powder, the onion powder, the mustard powder, and finally the cornflour. Next, mix the milk and the stock and add a little at a time to the onion mixture, until you have a smooth béchamel type sauce. Then add the white wine vinegar, the salt and pepper and the herbs, and pour the sauce over the chicken, sprinkling the Parmesan on top. Bake for 30 minutes, and serve with pasta, veg, potatoes, sweet potatoes, or rice.

Chicken and Tarragon Pie (CAN BE GLUTEN FREE)

Please don't go to the trouble of making your own flaky pastry- it's time consuming and unnecessary- even top chefs use the pre-made stuff these days! For me, this is the ultimate comfort food, and it's really shamelessly quick and easy to make. Serve with mashed potato for a deliciously luxurious treat. Again, you'll note that I'm using chicken thighs - it's a cheaper cut and so much tastier than chicken breast. Opt for gluten-free puff pastry if you want to make this gluten-free. Difficulty 5/10

Our testers said: "Oh my word. Lushhh. Vermouth is definitely an ingredient I will be experimenting with in the future - gives so much flavour to this pie without hindering it. I served it with Lamb's Lettuce."

Ingredients:

10 boned, skinned chicken thighs, cubed
1 medium onion, finely chopped
1 tbsp olive oil
1 sheet chilled puff pastry
1 egg, whisked with a fork
300ml double cream / Elmlea
200ml half white wine, half dry Vermouth
1 chicken stock cube in
250ml water
handful chopped tarragon

Preheat oven to 180°C. In a large frying pan, brown the chicken and the onion in the olive oil. Add the wine and Vermouth mix and simmer to reduce the volume by 2/3. Add the stock and reduce again by half. Add the cream and the tarragon and reduce again until slightly thickened. Add the pie mixture to a pie dish large enough for 4 servings and place the pastry on top (roll the pastry out if you need it to be bigger). Paint the egg over the top of the pastry to give it a lovely, glossy sheen when cooked. Cook for 30-35 minutes, or until golden brown.

CHICKEN & TARRAGON PIE

Chicken Enchiladas (CAN BE GLUTEN FREE)
Another super easy dish which always goes down extremely well with the family! When you're through with the neutropenic diet, this is great with a fresh, green salad, but in the meantime, you're still getting vitamins from the cooked peppers and onions. Opt for corn tortillas to make this gluten free. Difficulty 2/10

Our testers said: "Sheer simple bliss "

Ingredients:
1 pack of shop-bought wheat tortillas (2 per portion)
1 750g jar of Bolognese sauce (or similar - we're going easy on chilli here as stomachs may still be sensitive after HSCT)
8 skinless, boneless, chopped chicken breasts
1 of each - chopped and de-seeded red, orange, and yellow peppers
1 red onion, chopped
1 yellow onion, chopped
1 tbsp olive oil
300g mixed - grated Mozzarella and Monterey Jack cheese

Preheat oven to 180°C. Fry the chicken, peppers, and onions until thoroughly cooked. Add the Bolognese sauce and stir well to mix. Divide the mixture between the tortillas, fold over the sides to create a tortilla envelope shape and place them face up in a baking tray. Sprinkle with the cheese and bake for 15-20 minutes until golden and bubbling.

Chicken Korma (GLUTEN FREE)
A low fat version of the traditional korma, and you honestly wouldn't know this wasn't full of cream! James and Lucy both come back for seconds on this one. Difficulty: 4/10

Ingredients:
4 chicken breasts
coconut fry light or veg oil for frying
1 tbsp korma spices (I use: Old India Curry Powder Korma)
300ml Alpro coconut drink
4 tbsp Elmlea double (or double cream if you prefer)
chicken stock cube - crumbled a little semi skimmed milk
salt
2 tsp sugar or sweetener
1 tbsp cornflour
300g basmati rice

Alpro coconut drink/ water (for the rice)

Cut the chicken into chunks and brown in the fry light/ oil. Add the korma spices, then the cornflour. Add the salt and chicken stock cube. Add the coconut drink, the Elmlea and the sweetener. Taste and adjust seasoning if needed. Add a little semi- skimmed milk to thin the sauce down a little if needed. Cook the rice in the Alpro coconut drink and water.

Chicken Milanese with Neapolitan Spaghetti (CAN BE GLUTEN FREE)
Most definitely one of my favourites - so simple, but so tasty! James and I had this dish in Venice on a weekend away for my 40th birthday - I had to try and recreate it when we got home. To jazz it up, add some garlic powder and/or smoked paprika to the breadcrumbs. Delicious! You can use gluten free bread and pasta to easily make this gluten free. Difficulty 6/10

Our testers said: "Deliciously healthy, in an unfrustrating way!"

Ingredients:
4 chicken breasts
4 slices white bread, blitzed into breadcrumbs (or use ready-made)
2 eggs
400g dried spaghetti
cornflour for coating
salt and pepper to season breadcrumbs
4 tbsp extra virgin olive oil
1 tbsp garlic puree
1/2 tsp sugar/ sweetener
bunch of basil - finely chopped
1 400g tin of Italian chopped tomatoes
1 tsp Maldon salt
2 tbsp vegetable oil

Preheat oven to 180°C. Prepare the chicken as per the chicken Kyiv recipe at the start of this section (but without the garlic butter) - you may wish to flatten the fillets, so they are thinner and more like escalopes - it's personal choice. Dip them in the cornflour, then the egg, and then the seasoned breadcrumbs, then fry on either side in the vegetable oil for 2-3 minutes until golden brown, before transferring to the oven to cook for 25-30 minutes. While the chicken is cooking, put the pasta on to boil in a large pan of very salty water. Place the oil, garlic and basil in a saucepan and bring it to a slow sizzle (don't overcook the garlic or it will taste bitter). Add the tomatoes, Maldon salt and sugar, and cook on a high heat, stirring continuously. When the pasta is cooked, combine it with the sauce, and top with the chicken.

Chicken Mole aka Chilli Chocolate Chicken (GLUTEN FREE)

My take on 'Chicken Mole' - a dish I'd never heard of until a few years ago, but which has to be included as a tribute to HSCT in Mexico at Clinica Ruiz. It's a Mexican dish which uses chocolate, but this definitely isn't an authentic version, so I'm calling it Chilli Chocolate Chicken .. .Difficulty 5/10

Ingredients:
4 chicken breasts cut into chunks
1 400g tin mixed beans
1 400g tin chopped tomatoes
2 tbsp tomato puree
2 tsp smoked paprika
1 tsp mild chilli powder
1 tsp cumin
1 tsp cinnamon
1 onion chopped
1 red pepper, de-seeded and chopped
1 tsp garlic powder
1 tsp salt
200ml water
25g 85% dark chocolate
2 tsp cocoa powder blended in a little water
1 tbsp sugar/ sweetener

Brown the chicken, onion and pepper in a little oil or oil spray. Add the onion powder, garlic powder, smoked paprika, cumin, cinnamon and chilli powder and stir into the chicken mixture. Add the tomatoes, tomato puree, beans, salt, and water. Finally, stir in the chocolate, cocoa powder, and sweetener. Transfer the mixture to the slow cooker and cook on low for 6-7 hours. Serve with melted cheese, sour cream, nachos and/ or rice.

CHICKEN MOLE

Chicken Satay Skewers with Peanut Dipping Sauce (GLUTEN FREE) *Traditionally, this sauce should have chilli in it, but it still might be a bit soon for sensitive stomachs, so maybe avoid that for the time being. It's still packed with flavour, so you won't feel like you're missing out. We use wooden skewers for this but soak them in water for an hour or two beforehand.*
Difficulty 6/10

Ingredients:
8-10 chicken thigh fillets – diced
For the marinade:
2 tsp garlic puree
6 tbsp soy sauce
4 tbsp sesame oil
2 tsp maple syrup
red and yellow peppers - de-seeded and chopped
For the Satay Sauce:
2 tsp maple syrup
400ml coconut milk
splash of fish sauce
4 tbsp coconut oil
1 small onion - finely chopped
2 tsp garlic puree
300g smooth peanut butter
splash of soy sauce

Begin by marinating the chicken and peppers for at least 4hrs; blend together the garlic, soy sauce, sesame oil and maple syrup and coat the chicken thoroughly. Leave the marinade with the chicken in the fridge. While the chicken is marinating, make the satay sauce. Heat the coconut oil in a saucepan, over a low heat, and slowly sauté the onion and garlic paste (do this slowly so the garlic doesn't cook too fast and go bitter). Add the peanut butter & maple syrup, the splash of fish sauce and the splash of soy sauce. Combine all the ingredients together and stir continuously. Add the coconut milk and use a hand blender to incorporate this throughout the sauce. If desired, thin down the mixture with more coconut milk. When the chicken has been sufficiently marinated, thread it onto the skewers, along with the chopped peppers, and grill under a medium heat until brown, turning regularly - this should take 20-25 minutes. Serve the sauce, warm, on the side.

CHICKEN SATAY SKEWERS & PEANUT DIPPING SAUCE

Chicken and Pappardelle Pasta with a Creamy Pesto Sauce (CAN BE GLUTEN FREE) *Another easy, mid-week type of meal. Again, substitute the pasta for gluten free if required. Difficulty 2/10*

Our testers said: "Dead simple and toe-curlingly good! I reckon this could be good with cod fillets for pescatarians but reduce the oven cooking time by half. A stress-free recipe."

Ingredients:
4 chicken breasts
4 tbsp pesto
12 tbsp cream (I used Elmlea single light)
1 tbsp olive oil (I used oil spray)
1 chopped onion
1 tsp smoked paprika
salt and pepper
200ml chicken stock

Preheat oven to 180°C. Season the chicken with smoked paprika, and salt and pepper, then fry to brown each side, before baking for 30 minutes. Fry the onion, then add the pesto, cream, and stock, and reduce. Taste and season. Mix half the sauce with the pasta, then spoon the rest over the chicken when you place it on top.

Chilli Chicken Nachos (GLUTEN FREE)
What do you call cheese that doesn't belong to you? Nacho cheese!

I love this meal because it gives me a chance to tell that joke. Every. Single. Time. James absolutely loves that.

This one is so simple that it actually feels like a bit of a cheat...but it is one that we do have every now and again, and it always gets demolished. You can slow cook beef instead of using chicken or use roasted Mediterranean vegetables as they work equally well. At first, we just made this with beef, but we had friends round once who would only eat chicken, and this version was a big hit. Difficulty 4/10

Our testers said: "Sunshine on a plate this one."

Ingredients
4 chicken breasts, cubed
1 onion, chopped
1 400g tin cherry tomatoes
(these just work better than chopped tomatoes)
1 400g tin kidney beans
2 chicken/ vegetable stock cubes
1 red pepper - chopped
1 yellow pepper - chopped
1 green pepper - chopped
1 tsp mild chilli powder (or hot if you prefer!)
1 tsp smoked paprika
200ml water
1 large bag tortilla chips (opt for corn chips to make it gluten free)
200g good melting cheese such as Mozzarella or Monterey Jack

Pan fry the cubes of chicken and chopped onions and peppers, mix in the tinned goods, crumbled stock cubes, vegetables, and spices to make the chilli sauce (or use a shop bought sauce to make it easier). Bring to the boil and simmer for 20 minutes. Put the whole lot in a dish, on top of a bed of nachos, sprinkle with a good melting cheese, put it under the grill for a couple of minutes, and serve. We always have sour cream on the side. Also lovely with a salad - when that's allowed again. Be warned - there are never any leftovers!

CHILLI CHICKEN NACHOS

Creamy Garlic Chicken and Mushrooms (GLUTEN FREE)
I really do think that a slow cooker can be your new best friend when recovering from HSCT. If you can muster the energy to gather a load of ingredients together and put them in the slow cooker, you'll have a really tasty meal by dinnertime. I love lifting the lid off and smelling the aromas that come out of the pot ... Difficulty 4/10

Ingredients:
4 chicken breasts
300g mushrooms
400ml chicken / vegetable stock
2 tsp white wine vinegar
150ml Elmlea or double cream
1 onion – chopped
4 cloves garlic - finely chopped
1 tbsp cornflour
splash Worcester Sauce
1 tsp mustard powder
salt and pepper
oil / cooking spray /butter for frying

Season the chicken then brown in a frying pan on both sides and set aside. Brown the onions, mushrooms, and garlic. Add the cornflour and cook it in so you can't see any white. Add the stock a little at a time, then the Worcester sauce, mustard powder, salt and pepper and white wine vinegar. Finally add the cream and transfer, with the chicken, to a slow cooker. Cook for 3-4 hours on medium. Serve with rice, pasta, or potatoes.

Creamy Chicken and Tomato Gnocchi with Spinach
Vegetarian or non-vegetarian. The choice is yours with this one - the veggie option is listed separately later in the book. This one tastes very decadent and luxurious, but it's actually not too bad calorie-wise! Another easy one - you could make your own gnocchi, but a packet is so quick and easy. Difficulty 4/10

Our testers said: "Alison's Creamy Tomato and Spinach Gnocchi with Chicken is just delicious! The ricotta adds a lovely creamy effect without being too heavy, and the spinach gives off a tasty green flavour that enhances the thick sauce.
YUM!"
Ingredients:
4 chicken breasts gnocchi - 1 pack
1 large bag spinach
Red Leicester cheese (120g)
For the tomato sauce:
1 400g can chopped tomatoes (I really like Mutti tomatoes)
1 beef stock cube
1 tsp garlic salt
handful fresh chopped basil

splash of Worcester Sauce
2 tbsp dried mixed herbs
1 tbsp tomato puree
1 250g tub ricotta cheese

olive oil

seasoning

Preheat oven to 180°C. Combine the tomatoes, puree, salt, stock cube, herbs, and Worcester sauce. Heat on low until the sauce starts to become smooth. Add the ricotta cheese and blend (I use a stick blender) until fully combined and creamy.

Season the chicken and flash fry it in a frying pan on each side to brown it then drizzle with olive oil, add seasoning, and bake for 25-30 mins. When the chicken is done, cook the gnocchi - it's very fast, 2-3 mins. Drain it and add it to the tomato sauce, heating gently. Then add the spinach, a handful at a time, and let it wilt and be absorbed by the sauce before you add more - it can take a lot of spinach! Sprinkle with the Red Leicester cheese and put it back in the oven for 5 minutes or until the cheese melts. Top with the chicken and serve.

CREAMY CHICKEN & TOMATO GNOCCHI WITH SPINACH

Creamy Chicken Crepes (CAN BE GLUTEN FREE)

Fanny Cradock (formidable TV chef from the 50s-70s) once said "If your crepes are thick enough to toss, you should toss them out of the window..." So, yes, this is my recipe for crepes. Specifically, crepes with a creamy chicken, mushroom, and tarragon sauce. And thin - they need to be thin. Use gluten free flour instead of plain wheat flour to make this gluten free. Make it even easier by buying ready-made crepes. Makes 3 crepes each. Difficulty 3/10

Our testers said: "Really delicious and very more-ish."

Ingredients:
4 chicken breasts cut into bite sized chunks
200g white button mushrooms - cut in half
1 tbsp tarragon
1 tbsp cornflour
4 tbsp single cream
100ml milk mixed with a stock cube and 100ml boiling water (I used a chicken stock cube)
oil for frying
seasoning
For the batter:
2 eggs
100g plain flour
300ml milk
oil for cooking

This should produce around 500ml of batter - you want to allow just over 40ml of batter for each pancake. Cook the chicken, tarragon, and mushrooms in the oil. Add the cornflour and mix it in until it's absorbed. Add the stock/milk mixture a bit at a time and cook down until you have a thick sauce. Taste and season. Stir in the cream just before plating up. Mix the milk, eggs, and flour for the batter, and measure out 40ml of the batter for each crepe and fry until golden, turning halfway through. Fill the crepes with the chicken/mushroom mix and dust with smoked paprika.

CREAMY CHICKEN CREPES

Crunchy Coconut Chicken (CAN BE GLUTEN FREE)
A favourite of James's, this one feels a bit takeaway-ish without actually being a takeaway Panko is typically wheat based, but I believe you can also buy gluten free panko online. Difficulty: 4/10

Our testers said: "We devoured the lot! Beautiful Finger Food!"

Ingredients:
4 chicken breasts cut into strips
Cornflour for dusting
75g panko
50g desiccated coconut
1/2 tsp salt
1/2 tsp msg (optional)
coconut cooking spray/ vegetable oil
2 eggs

Preheat the oven to 180°C. Whisk the eggs and place in a bowl. Coat the chicken strips in the cornflour, then dip them in the egg. Mix the coconut with the panko and the salt and coat the chicken pieces in the mixture. Place the chicken pieces on a baking tray, spray with coconut oil spray (if available - otherwise drizzle with oil), and cook for 30-35 minutes, turning halfway through. Serve with chips and a sweet chilli dip or mayonnaise.

CRUNCHY COCONUT CHICKEN

Crunchy Jerk Chicken (CAN BE GLUTEN FREE)
Spice up your life! This is probably about as spicy as I'll go, having a severe aversion to chilli! Opt for gluten free bread to make this gluten free. Difficulty 4/10

Our tasters said: "Really tasty!"

4 chicken breasts cut into strips
4 slices wholemeal bread whizzed into breadcrumbs (approx 200g)
2 eggs, whisked
2 tsp jerk seasoning (I use Barts)
1 tbsp vegetable oil / oil spray
4 sweet potatoes
1 tsp garlic powder

Preheat oven to 200°C. Chop the sweet potatoes into chunks (skin on is fine as they're going to be cooked, but give them a wash first), then sprinkle them with the garlic powder and drizzle with oil. These will want about 45 minutes in a hot oven, turning once or twice, and I like to finish them under the grill to crisp them up a bit. Mix the breadcrumbs with the Cajun spice. Dunk the chicken strips in the egg, then the breadcrumb mix. Brown the strips briefly in a pan then place on a baking tray and cook for 30 minutes at 180°C turning half way through.
Some corn on the cob would go nicely with this dish.

Dill and Coriander Chicken with Broccoli, Onion, and Spinach Pasta. (CAN BE GLUTEN FREE)
Dill and Coriander are both strong flavours, but they match well in this dish. As usual, gluten free pasta will make this a gluten free option. Difficulty 3/10
Ingredients:
2 chicken breasts
1 tsp fine sea salt
1/2 tsp ground black pepper
handful of dill, finely chopped
handful of coriander, finely chopped
150g pasta
1 head of broccoli
300g spinach
1 onion, chopped
olive oil

Preheat oven to 180°C. Mix the salt, pepper and herbs and rub them into both sides of the chicken breasts. Bake for 30 minutes. Fry the onion until browned then add the spinach to wilt a little at a time. At the same time, cook the pasta and broccoli together (add the broccoli for the last 5 minutes) and drain. Mix the pasta, spinach, onion, and broccoli together and drizzle with olive oil. Top with the chicken.

Fakeaway Spicy Crunchy Chicken (CAN BE GLUTEN FREE)
Can't take the credit for this one. I've tried loads of takeaway spice combinations for KFC and this one is the closest it gets, I've found. (It has got my spin on it though because it's not deep fried - still works just as well). I make up this mixture and keep it in an airtight tub to use when I need it - it makes a lot. You'll get several goes out of one batch of it. You only need about 3 tablespoons of it to make 12 chicken thighs.

Opt for Gluten Free flour for a gluten free choice. Difficulty: 6/10

Ingredients:
12 boneless chicken thighs
oil / oil spray
Spice mix:
2/3 tbsp salt
1/2 tbsp dried thyme
1/2 tbsp dried basil
1/3 tbsp dried oregano
1 tbsp celery salt
1 tbsp black pepper
1 tbsp mustard powder
4 tbsp paprika
2 tbsp garlic salt
1 tbsp ground ginger
3 tbsp white pepper
all mixed with 140g plain flour

Preheat oven to 180°C. Coat 12 chicken thighs in cornflour (1 tablespoon is fine for this bit), then the egg, then the spice/flour mix, and brown on both sides with fry light or oil in a frying pan. Transfer to an oven dish, spray with fry light or drizzle with oil, and cook for 20-25 minutes, turning halfway through, until cooked throughout.

FAKEAWAY SPICY CRUNCHY CHICKEN

Fusion Chicken (GLUTEN FREE)
This is an east meets west sort of dish. Lots of zingy Mediterranean flavours, but with a little heat just a little). Dead easy too, as you only need a roasting pan. Difficulty: 2/10

Our testers said: 'A surprising combo of ingredients that go really well together! Really good, very innovative, and imaginative. Perhaps Tofu or potatoes to replace chicken for vegetarians. "

Ingredients:
4 chicken breasts, chopped (thighs would work equally well)
2 red peppers, chopped
1 onion, chopped
3 tbsp maple syrup (I use honey usually, and I'd recommend that, but maple syrup is a good substitute as honey isn't allowed on a neutropenic diet)
3 tsp garam masala
1/2 tsp ground black pepper
2 tsp turmeric
1 tsp smoked paprika
1 lemon - juice and zest
1 lime - juice and zest
250g halloumi – sliced

Preheat oven to 180°C. Mix everything together, put it in an oven dish, put it in the oven for 40 minutes, turning halfway through. It's that easy! Serve with rice.

Hunter's Chicken (GLUTEN FREE)

Who doesn't love a smoky, BBQ hunters chicken with bacon and cheese? Staple of the great British Pub Lunch. This is my version ...Use a jar of BBQ sauce if you prefer to make this easier. Difficulty 4/10

Our testers said: "So good! I loved the sauce!"
Ingredients:
4 chicken breasts
4 smoked bacon medallions/ rashers
200g grated cheddar/ mozzarella
For the BBQ sauce:
1 400g tin tomatoes
2 tbsp tomato puree
1 tbsp sugar / sweetener
1 tbsp white wine vinegar
2 tsp Worcester Sauce
1 tsp onion powder
1 tsp garlic powder
1 tsp smoked paprika
pinch of salt

Preheat oven to 180°C. Layer the bacon medallions onto the chicken breasts and place in an oven proof dish. Cook for 25-30 minutes or until the chicken is cooked and the bacon is beginning to crisp. Put all the remaining ingredients (except the cheese) in a saucepan and bring to the boil. At this point, I get a stick blender in there as it makes it nice and smooth. Now pour the sauce on and around the chicken and bacon and sprinkle the cheese on the top. Put it back in the oven for a further ten minutes. Serve it with chips, mash, rice, pasta - whatever takes your fancy.

HUNTER'S CHICKEN

LEMON CHICKEN

Lemon Chicken (GLUTEN FREE)
This recipe came about as a quick, tasty recipe for a small dinner party. The sweet and sour flavours complement each other perfectly. Difficulty 4/10

Our testers said: "Tangy and toe-curlingly good, this one!"
Ingredients:
4 chicken breasts
2 tbsp cornflour
1 tsp MSG (optional)
1 tbsp cornflour for sauce
4 spring onions chopped finely
chicken stock 800ml
juice and zest of 2 lemons
1 tsp fish sauce
1 tsp rice wine
sugar / sweetener to taste
yellow food colouring (optional)

Cut the chicken into strips and coat in the cornflour. Brown the chicken in a large pan or wok with some msg and the spring onions. Set the chicken and spring onions aside. Add the stock to the pan and reduce by half. Add a teaspoon of rice wine and a teaspoon of fish sauce. Add the lemon juice and zest, and the cornflour (blended with a little cold water) to thicken. Now taste it. I added 2-3 tablespoons of sweetener, but you might want it sweeter/ more bitter so add it a little at a time and keep tasting it until it's right for you. Add some yellow food colouring to get the vibrant lemony colour. Re-add the chicken and bring it all back to the boil. You could garnish with more spring onions when you aren't neutropenic. Serve with egg fried rice.

Mozzarella Stuffed Pancetta Wrapped Chicken (GLUTEN FREE)
You can, of course, purchase a version of this in most supermarkets - but with this one you get none of the additives, and you control the portion sizes - and it really doesn't take much longer than it does to get a shop bought one out of the packaging. Difficulty 4/10

Ingredients:
4 chicken breasts
8 slices Parma ham or pancetta
12 basil leaves 300g
Mozzarella
olive oil

Preheat oven to 180°C. Slice the Mozzarella into 16 slices.

Using a sharp knife, slice into the widest side of a chicken breast, making a pocket. Push three of the Mozzarella slices into each pocket. Then put three whole basil leaves over that, before wrapping each chicken breast in two slices of the ham. Place the last 4 pieces of Mozzarella on the top.

Place in an oven dish, drizzle with olive oil, and cook for 30-35 minutes. I serve this with smoked paprika potatoes and carrots - I parboil thin slices of potato, cool and brown briefly in a frying pan before transferring to a hot oven to crisp up. Steam some carrots then add them to a frying pan with a little butter or oil, add a splash of white wine, and brown.

MOZZARELLA STUFFED PANCETTA WRAPPED CHICKEN

Pan Fried Duck Breast with Blackberry Jus (GLUTEN FREE)
The trick is to start the duck in a cold pan, get a good crisp on the skin, which takes about 5-7 minutes, then put it in the oven to finish it off. Practice makes perfect! I like crispy skin on fish too and it took me ages to discover that it will release itself from the pan if you're patient with it - there were many instances of demolished fish from my turning it way too soon! Difficulty 7/10

Ingredients:
4 duck breasts
300g blackberries
2 tbsp caster sugar / sweetener
1 shallot, finely chopped
200ml red wine
200ml chicken stock
4 thyme sprigs
2 tsp juniper berries, crushed

Preheat oven to 180°C. Score the skin of the duck breasts in a criss-cross pattern and season. Place them skin-side down in a cold frying pan and set over a medium heat. Cook for 20 minutes, tipping the excess fat out of the pan as it cooks.

Meanwhile, put the blackberries in a small saucepan with the sugar and simmer for 5 minutes, crushing the berries with the back of a fork; set aside. When most of the fat from the duck has rendered and the skin is golden and crisp, turn the breasts over and cook the flesh side for 2 minutes, then transfer to a roasting tray and place in the oven for 15-20 minutes until cooked through (not pink - sorry). Remove from the oven, wrap loosely in foil, and rest them. While the duck breasts are resting, spoon all but 1 tbsp fat out of the pan. Set the pan over a medium-low heat and cook the shallot in the fat for 2-3 minutes, until softened.

Add the wine, stock, thyme and juniper berries to the pan and simmer for 5 minutes over a high heat, until reduced and syrupy. Remove the thyme. Stir in the blackberries and any resting juices from the duck and simmer until warmed through. Slice the duck and serve with the sauce, plus some steamed green vegetables and potatoes, if desired.

PAN FRIED DUCK BREAST WITH BLACKBERRY JUS

Roast Poussin (GLUTEN FREE)

I love this because it's so versatile - the poussin gets a different flavour every time I cook it - this one is garlic and Mediterranean herbs (I usually serve it with dauphinoise potatoes and green beans). This is one of those that you can do for a midweek dinner or for guests - always goes down well and looks like much more work than it actually is. Difficulty 5/10

Ingredients:
4 poussin
For the coating:
4 tsp garlic puree
handful basil, finely chopped
handful oregano, finely chopped
1 tsp fine sea salt
1 chicken stock cube, crumbled
1 tbsp olive oil

Preheat oven to 180°C. Mix all the ingredients for the coating together and rub into the poussin. Cook for 50 minutes, or until thoroughly cooked throughout, and allow to rest for ten minutes before serving.

Salt and Pepper Chicken (GLUTEN FREE)

This salt and pepper chicken would go well with rice or noodles but is also really nice with some cheese and chive mash, along with a bit of white cabbage.
Difficulty 2/10

Our testers said: "Tasty recipe and so easy!"

Ingredients:
4 chicken breasts
1 tsp ground black pepper
2 tsp fine sea salt
1 tsp Chinese five spice
1 tsp MSG (optional)

Preheat oven to 180°C. Mix the dry ingredients together and rub into both sides of the chicken breasts. Seal the chicken on both sides in a hot pan, then cook for 25 mins. Serve with whatever you fancy!

Spinach, Garlic, and Herb Chicken Pasta (CAN BE GLUTEN FREE)
Another quick and easy midweek meal - from hob to plate in 30 minutes. Change the pasta for gluten free, if desired. Difficulty 4/10

Ingredients:
4 chicken breasts
200g spinach
220g dried pasta
6 garlic cloves thinly sliced
olive oil
salt and pepper

Preheat oven to 180°C. Start by seasoning, then browning the chicken on both sides in a frying pan. After about 15 mins, add the garlic and cook for another 15-20 minutes (you don't want the garlic to get bitter and crunchy, so after 15 mins or so should be fine). Cook the pasta. For a neutropenic diet I'd steam the spinach thoroughly. Nowadays I just stir it into the hot, drained pasta until it wilts. Set the chicken aside and add all the garlic to the pasta, with a drizzle of olive oil. Plate up, placing the chicken on top.

Sticky Chinese Chicken (GLUTEN FREE)
Yet another takeaway style dish that delivers what it promises. Great for a weekend treat! Difficulty 3/10

Our testers said "Use ready chopped garlic and ginger if fine motor skills are a problem."

Ingredients:
8 boneless skinless chicken thighs
4 spring onions chopped
4 large cloves garlic chopped finely
2 inches fresh ginger chopped finely
4 tbsp cornflour
1 tsp salt
1 tsp MSG (optional)
1 tsp sesame oil
For the sauce.
Combine:
2 tbsp maple syrup
2 tbsp dark soy sauce
1 tsp rice wine
1 tbsp tomato puree
2 tsp sugar/ sweetener

Cut the chicken thighs into pieces.

Combine the cornflour, salt and MSG and coat the chicken in it. Add the oil to the pan and get it hot. Add the coated chicken. When it is starting to brown, add the garlic, ginger, and spring onions. Continue cooking until the chicken is golden brown and cooked through.

Add the sauce ingredients and cook until the chicken absorbs them and is sticky. Serve with egg fried rice.

STICKY CHINESE CHICKEN

Sticky Salted Caramel Chicken (GLUTEN FREE)

This probably shouldn't work, but it really does...it was inspired by a chain hotel's restaurant that I used to frequent on work trips. A version of this was on their menu, so I had to work out a recipe of my own. Difficulty 3/10 Our tasters said "It shouldn't work...but it tastes sooo good!"

Ingredients:
12 skinless boneless chicken thighs
oil for frying
1 tbsp cornflour
1 tsp smoked paprika
1 tsp garlic powder
1 tsp salt
1 tablespoon salted caramel syrup / sauce of your choice

Preheat oven to 180°C. Cut the chicken into pieces. Mix the dry ingredients together and dredge the chicken in it, before browning in a hot frying pan. Transfer to an oven proof dish and drizzle with the salted caramel. Mix thoroughly and cook in the oven for 20-25 minutes, turning a couple of times. This would go nicely with crispy potatoes, but we have also had it with orzo pasta with spinach, basil, crème fraîche, and a bit of chicken stock.

Sticky Sesame Chicken (GLUTEN FREE)

Fakeaway fabulousness that's great as a weekend treat. Difficulty 4/10

4 chicken breasts

For the marinade:
2 tbsp maple syrup
1 tbsp soy sauce
1 tbsp fish sauce
1/2 tsp sesame oil
2 tbsp sesame seeds (toasted - you'll need to do this yourself, I think. I've never seen ready toasted sesame seeds on sale. Just put them in a dry frying pan and keep turning until they get some colour.)
For the sauce:
2 cloves garlic - chopped
2 tbsp maple syrup
2 tbsp soy sauce
2 tbsp rice wine vinegar
1 tbsp fish sauce

Cut the chicken into chunks and soak in the marinade for a couple of hours. When it's had a couple of hours, add the chicken chunks from the marinade to a hot pan, and cook through - it's best to do this in a couple of batches so the pan doesn't get overcrowded. Set the chicken to one side. Using the same pan, add the garlic, fish sauce, maple syrup, soy sauce and rice wine vinegar and cook until it becomes thick and syrupy. Put the cooked chicken back in the sticky sauce and add half of the toasted sesame seeds. Serve with egg fried rice and sprinkle the remaining toasted sesame seeds over the chicken.

STICKY SESAME CHICKEN

Sweet Chilli, Garlic, and Ginger Chicken (GLUTEN FREE)

Being unfeasibly sensitive to chilli, I have to go sparingly - but this one is tolerable even for me. Feel free to add extra chilli jam or even some cooked, fresh chillies. Difficulty 2/10

Our testers said: "Really easy and quick to make. This should work with a nice firm fish fillet for pescatarians. Lip-smackingly good!"

Ingredients:
3 chicken breasts
3 tbsp plain yoghurt (not bio, added good bacteria or probiotic)
1 tsp ground ginger
1 tsp dried coriander (or a handful of fresh, chopped)
1 tsp sweet chilli sauce or chilli jam (add more if you can tolerate it - unlike me!!)
1 tsp garlic puree

Preheat oven to 180°C. Mix the yoghurt, coriander, chilli sauce, ginger, and garlic together and coat the chicken with it on both sides. If you have time, let this marinate for a few hours, but no problem if not. Cook in the oven for 30 minutes. Serve with noodles and stir fry veg.

Tandoori Chicken Kebabs (GLUTEN FREE)

This one always goes down really well in our house and you can switch it up a bit by changing the meat/veg. Try mushrooms, lamb, king prawns, or firm white fish... Difficulty 5/10

Ingredients:
4 chicken breasts - cubed
1 of each - red, yellow, orange, green pepper
- cut into square chunks
Spice mix:
2 tsp cumin
2 tsp coriander powder
1 tsp ground black pepper
1 tsp turmeric
1 tsp ground nutmeg
4 tsp paprika
2 tsp mustard powder
1 tsp ground ginger
2 crushed garlic cloves
1 tsp cinnamon
2 tsp maple syrup
2 tbsp tomato puree
1 tsp garlic salt

Water to thin the marinade down a bit - around 50ml

Preheat the oven to 180°C. Marinate the chicken and peppers in the spice mix for a few hours then thread the chunks onto skewers, along with the peppers. Cook for 30-40 minutes in the oven, turning half way.

TANDOORI KEBABS

Thai Green Chicken (GLUTEN FREE)
Now this isn't a fully authentic one - but there are still a couple of unusual but really crucial ingredients in this that really make the dish. One is dried shrimp (it smells utterly disgusting, so hold your nose), and galangal which is a bit like citrusy ginger, so don't compromise on those things. You can easily just buy a jar of Thai green curry paste, but fresh is much nicer - and you can control the heat this way. So do feel free to add lots of Thai chilli if you want to. For me this is just right. Difficulty 8/10

Ingredients:
12 chicken thighs cut into thirds
600ml Alpro coconut drink (or other coconut milk)
1 tsp fish sauce
16 new potatoes cut in half
150g green beans
For the paste:
3 spring onions, roughly chopped
4 cloves of garlic
zest of one lime, plus half the juice
1 tsp ground coriander
1 tsp ground cumin
1/2 tsp turmeric
1/2 tsp black pepper
1/2 tsp cayenne pepper
small bunch of coriander - stalks and leaves
handful Thai basil
2 tsp dried shrimp paste
1 tsp galangal
A little water to thin the paste down

Put all the paste ingredients in a blender. Blend. That's the hardest bit of this one! Fry the chicken pieces in a little coconut oil, then add a couple of tablespoons of the paste (you'll get a good couple of portions out of this). **Don't be tempted to lick the spoon - the dried prawns are raw so the paste must be cooked.** When the paste has cooked, add the coconut milk and the fish sauce, and stir it all together. This isn't meant to be a thick sauce, so don't feel you have to thicken it up. In the meantime, boil the potatoes for about 5 minutes, then add the beans for another 3-4 minutes. Drain and add them to the chicken. You could have rice or noodles with this, but with the beans and potatoes I think it's already plenty.

THAI GREEN CHICKEN CURRY

Thyme and Juniper Duck with Mushroom Risotto (GLUTEN FREE)
Duck, mushrooms, thyme, and juniper berries are flavours that go together so well, and this recipe uses all of them. Difficulty 7/10

Our testers said: "This is such a classy dish. The flavours all meld together into something that I can only describe as "surprisingly obvious". Maybe an aubergine sliced in half lengthways and scored diagonally flesh-side, then seasoned and cooked in same way as duck breast... would replace meat for vegetarians. "

Ingredients:
4 duck breasts
bunch thyme
1 dstspn spoon dried juniper berries
1.5 litres stock (chicken or vegetable)
400g sliced mushrooms
1 sliced onion
2 tsp garlic powder
300g risotto rice
200ml white wine
salt and pepper
1 tbsp crème fraîche

Preheat the oven to 180°C. Grind/blend the thyme and the juniper berries and rub half of this mixture into the duck with salt and pepper. In a **cold** pan, place seasoned duck breasts, skin side down, and cook for around 5 minutes until the fat is rendered and golden brown. Turn and seal for a minute on the other side. Set aside. Drain off the excess oil from the pan and fry the mushrooms, onion, the remainder of the thyme and juniper mix, and the garlic powder, until browned. Put the mushroom and onion mixture in a large saucepan and add the risotto rice. Stir for a couple of minutes, on a low heat, until the rice is starting to become transparent. Then add the white wine and stir until it's absorbed. Add the stock a ladleful at a time (you might not need it all) adding more each time it's absorbed - keep stirring it. It will take around 20 minutes to cook. After the first five minutes, put the duck in the oven at 180°C for 20-30 minutes until thoroughly cooked through and not pink. When the rice is cooked, taste and season it, add a tablespoon of crème fraîche and mix it in.

THYME AND JUNIPER DUCK WITH MUSHROOM RISOTTO

Meat

Beef Stew and Dumplings

A super easy one that you can place it in the slow cooker for 6-7 hours, or in the oven as I've done here. You can make your own suet dumplings from scratch if you want to, but I think the easier option is totally justified here, so go for a packet of dumpling mix to make it easier on yourself! Difficulty 3/10

Our testers said: "Fantastic 10 out of 10. Cook low and slow, 2 red onions added and cooked carrots, cabbage and peas for other half and went down a treat.
We'll definitely have this again."

Ingredients:
1 red onion
500g diced neck of beef
3 large, chopped, peeled potatoes,
1 tbsp cornflour
1 pint strong beef stock
salt & pepper
ready-made dumpling mix

Preheat the oven to 170°C. Brown the beef and onion in a frying pan, then add the cornflour, before pouring over strong beef stock and adding to a casserole dish. I cooked it at 170°C for 1 hour, 50 mins, stirring occasionally, then added the dumplings for 20 minutes more. To make the dumplings from a packet mix you generally just add a bit of water to make a dough, then divide into balls.

Really very little work but very tasty!

BEEF STEW & DUMPLINGS

Beef With Green Pepper In Black Bean Sauce (GLUTEN FREE)
Another takeaway dish that's way nicer than anything you could get out of a jar! Worth choosing a few of these dishes and batch cooking them so you have them in the freezer for a takeaway night - also a really handy thing to do BEFORE you have HSCT. Difficulty 5/10

Best in a slow cooker
Ingredients:
500g minute steak, sliced into bite sized pieces
1 green pepper, chopped
3 spring onions, chopped
2 beef stock cubes in 400ml boiling water
4 garlic cloves, chopped finely
2-inch chunk of ginger, chopped finely
1 400g tin black beans
1 tbsp rice wine
2 tsp fish sauce
1 tbsp sugar / sweetener
1 tbsp cornflour
salt to taste
oil for frying

Fry the steak, garlic, ginger, spring onions and green pepper in the oil, until the steak is browned. Add the black beans. Add the cornflour and stir until it is absorbed. Add the fish sauce and rice wine to the beef stock and pour this into the beef mixture. Add the sugar/ sweetener and transfer to the slow cooker.

Cook on medium for 2-3 hours - it is cooked prior to this stage, but I think it really benefits from a couple of hours in the slow cooker to let the flavours infuse. Adjust the seasoning if necessary. Serve with egg fried rice.

BEEF IN GREEN PEPPER AND BLACK BEAN SAUCE

Braised Beef Tagliatelle (CAN BE GLUTEN FREE)
James and I love this one, but my youngest daughter prefers an exclusively tomato sauce with pasta ("This is a bit too much like gravy"), so you can omit the stock cube made up with water and swap it for a 400g tin of chopped tomatoes if you prefer. Again, use Gluten Free pasta for a gluten-free version. Difficulty 4/10

Our testers said: "This was jam-packed with flavour - loved it. The veg are all finely grated but add to the oomph in the sauce."

Best in a slow cooker
Ingredients:
500g diced stewing steak/ braising beef
salt and pepper
1 tbsp olive oil
1 onion chopped
4 cloves garlic chopped
1 stick celery finely grated
1 carrot finely grated
200g button mushrooms
handful of fresh thyme leaves
1 tbsp cornflour
1 beef stock cube (dry)
1 beef stock cube made up with 1 pint boiling water
1/2 tbsp tomato puree
splash Worcester sauce
1X glass red wine (125ml to 250ml. I'm not going to lie to you - I go for 250)
1/4 tsp ground black pepper
salt to taste
8-12 balls dried Tagliatelle
Parmesan to sprinkle on the top (to taste)

Season the beef and fry in the oil. Add the onions, celery, garlic, and carrot and cook down until the veg is very soft. Add the thyme and one of the beef stock cubes, crumbled. Add the cornflour and mix in until you can no longer see any white (it will look like a mushy mess at this point, but it's fine, have faith). Set the mixture aside. Use the red wine to de-glaze the pan and then add the tomato puree, Worcester sauce and the other stock cube dissolved in a pint of water.

Bring the liquid to the boil. Add the meat and veg mix, plus the button mushrooms, to the slow cooker, plus the black pepper, and stir the liquid in well. Cook on low for 6-7 hours. Keep checking on it and add more water if it needs thinning at any point. Add salt at the end if it needs it. Serve with the Tagliatelle. Spoon a few scoops of the ragu into the pasta and mix it in, then add more to the top, plus a sprinkling of Parmesan cheese.

BRAISED BEEF TAGLIATELLE

Cheats' Carbonara (CAN BE GLUTEN FREE)

When I was a very small child, my mother tells me, I would eat nothing but bacon, eggs, and cheese - so it stands to reason that this is absolutely my favourite dish in the world. In fact, it was the first dish I ever cooked for James, and I probably still eat it at least once a month!

However, an authentic Spaghetti Carbonara contains very lightly cooked egg yolks - and these are a no on a neutropenic diet. Parmesan, although usually unpasteurised, is actually ok. So, this is my cheats' version, which uses cream instead - and it's every bit as good from a 'comfort food' perspective. For a vegan version, cook sliced mushrooms in olive oil and smoked paprika, along with a little vegetable stock with soya cream. Use Gluten Free spaghetti for a gluten free version. Difficulty 4/10

Ingredients:
400g spaghetti
200ml double cream
160g Parmesan cheese grated
150g Red Leicester cheese grated (I know. This cheese has no business in a carbonara, does it? Trust me!)
16 rashers streaky smoked bacon - cooked and cut into pieces.

Cook the pasta and drain. Add the cream, Red Leicester cheese, bacon and 3/4 of the Parmesan to the pasta. Heat on a very low heat until the cheese melts into the cream - stir constantly until it's a smooth sauce. Serve with the remainder of the Parmesan sprinkled on top.

CHEATS' CARBONARA

CHEESEBURGER

Cheeseburgers (and Meatballs!) GLUTEN FREE
This makes 4 burgers and about 25 meatballs for another day. The mixture of pork and beef makes the burgers extra tasty and juicy. The smoked paprika and the Stubbs Liquid Smoke give the burgers a nice smoky taste. Difficulty 5/10

Ingredients:
500g pork mince
500g beef mince
handful thyme
handful parsley
handful oregano
2 tsp smoked paprika
1 tsp salt
1/2 tsp pepper
1 tsp MSG (optional)
2 tsp Stubbs Liquid Smoke (optional - available online)
2 eggs
1 tbsp cornflour
flour for shaping
oil for frying

Preheat the oven to 220°C for the chips. Chop all the herbs finely then combine all the ingredients together.

Take out 4 tennis ball sized portions of the mixture and shape into patties on a floured surface. Shape the remainder of the mixture into meatballs - you should get 4 burgers and around 25 meatballs.

Fry the burgers in the oil, turning often, for 10-12 minutes. Serve on a regular or gluten free toasted bun (omit the salad shown in the picture, but condiments are fine) and cheese slices.

I'd serve this with healthy chips - the chips are parboiled before being sprayed with fry light, then cooked for around 45 mins in a hot oven.

Chilli (CAN BE GLUTEN FREE)
As mentioned previously, I'm VERY sensitive to chilli and can't tolerate much of it at all - especially the fresh stuff, so mine is very mild and just uses powder - add more, to taste, if you like it hot, and feel free to add in some fresh chillies too. Use corn tortillas to make this a Gluten Free option. Difficulty 5/10

Our testers said: "The homemade nachos. With the homemade flavourings. What a superb idea. Gives an authenticity to this classic dish!"

Ingredients:
500g minced beef (though it's really lovely with stewing steak too)
1 onion, chopped
1 400g tin cherry tomatoes (these just seem to work better than chopped tomatoes)
1 400g tin kidney beans
2 beef stock cubes
1 tsp mild chilli powder (or hot if you prefer)
1 tsp smoked paprika
250ml water
200g Red Leicester cheese/ Monterey Jack cheese
For the nachos:
4 soft flour wraps
garlic fry light/ garlic oil
1 tsp smoked paprika
1 tsp salt
1 tsp garlic powder

Preheat the oven to 190°C. Brown the mince and onions and add the smoked paprika, the beef stock cubes and the chilli powder, and stir to combine. Add the cherry tomatoes and the kidney beans, and finally the water. Cook on low in a slow cooker for six hours. To make the nachos: You can, of course, just open a bag - but these are much nicer, lovely, and warm, and you can play around with the seasoning. Spray both sides of the wraps with garlic fry light, or brush with garlic oil, then slice them into triangles. Bake for ten minutes, turning halfway through. Combine the smoked paprika, salt and garlic powder and season the nachos with the powder when they're done. Serve with rice and the Red Leicester cheese or Monterey Jack cheese, and a dollop of sour cream or crème fraîche.

CHILLI

Corned Beef "Mash" (GLUTEN FREE)

This is another super easy, comforting, warming autumn dish. I make no apology for the simplicity of this one! I know it's supposed to be hash, with lumpier potatoes, but there's something about the smooth mash that makes it more comforting. Difficulty 3/10

Ingredients:
8 large potatoes - boiled, mashed, and seasoned (add cream, butter, whatever you like)
1 chopped onion - fried
1 400g tin corned beef
1 tsp Dijon mustard
200g grated cheese (Red Leicester, Cheddar, Mozzarella - whatever you like as long as it's a neutropenic-friendly one)

Preheat the oven to 180°C. Mix all of the ingredients (except the cheese) together. Put it in a large oven proof dish, sprinkle the cheese on top, and bake for 20-25 minutes. Serve with red cabbage and crusty bread (I love it with an extra dollop of Dijon mustard).

David and Zia Paola's Spaghetti Bolognese (CAN BE GLUTEN FREE)
My Aunt Paola is Italian, and this is the recipe my Mum always used from when I was a small child. 'Zia' is Italian for Aunt, so that's what we call her. Uncle David is no longer with us, but Zia Paola is still going strong at 87! Again, substitute the pasta for gluten free if desired.

Our tasters said: "Well worth the slow simmering - makes for a very flavoursome sauce. No Campbell's Consommé available in this part of the world, so I used strong beef stock instead. An aubergine/mushroom combo, diced, could be tabby for vegetarians. So good to try a real family recipe with a story behind it."

Ingredients:
1 packet of spaghetti
1/2 onion, chopped finely
1 carrot finely grated
1 stick of celery - minced
500g minced meat
(the best mix is three parts minced beef to one-part minced pork).
1 or 2 glasses of red wine
1 120ml can of Campbell's Consommé
1 beef stock cube (optional)
2 fat cloves of garlic - minced
1/4 to 1/2 tube tomato puree
mushrooms (optional)
sprig rosemary or mixed herbs to taste (Paola uses oregano)

salt and pepper
2 tsp vegetable oil
Parmesan cheese to flavour.

Fry onion in oil until just golden. Turn down the heat, add the garlic, carrot, and celery, but don't allow it to brown. Add meat and mix and fry until the colour changes. Add puree, diluted in the wine, and the consommé. Add stock cube and herbs. Simmer very gently for at least an hour, stirring occasionally. Check flavour and seasoning and adjust accordingly (salt etc). Add more wine if necessary, and mushrooms if desired. Simmer for at least one more hour- the longer the better, and to be honest, I like to put the whole lot in a slow cooker and leave it there all day at this point - but keep an eye on consistency. Cook the spaghetti in fast boiling water. Drain in a colander and pour boiling water over it to remove starch. For an authentic presentation, put some of the sauce into a big frying pan on a low heat. Add the cooked spaghetti and mix until completely covered. Add the rest of the meat sauce and mix well. Heat gently until the sauce is dry enough. Add cheese to flavour and serve.

UNCLE DAVID AND ZIA PAOLA'S SPAGHETTI BOLOGNESE

Goulash (GLUTEN FREE)

I was chatting with my mum about our Polish heritage recently and was inspired to make goulash for dinner that night. I first had this when I visited Poland nearly 30 years ago, and it's lovely with some buttered cabbage or mashed potatoes - or just some crusty bread. Not forgetting a good dollop of sour cream on the top. Bags of flavour and especially lovely on a chilly autumn night. Difficulty 4/10

Our testers said" A really heart-warming meal to come back to this afternoon. The acidity of a yoghurt garnish really complements the smokey hues of the sauce. I served this with fresh tagliatelle."

Best in a slow cooker
Serves 4-6
Ingredients:
1kg diced braising steak
1 tbsp oil
1 onion chopped
4 cloves garlic finely chopped
1 red pepper chopped
1 400g tin chopped tomatoes
4 tbsp tomato puree
1 tsp sugar
2 stock cubes in 400ml water
150ml red wine
1 tbsp cornflour
2 tsp caraway seeds
1 tbsp paprika
2 tbsp smoked paprika
salt and pepper
crème fraîche / sour cream / plain yoghurt

Season the beef and brown. Transfer to a slow cooker. Add the caraway seeds to the pan and toast them. Add the red wine and cook down for a couple of minutes. Transfer to a slow cooker. Add the onions, garlic, red pepper and cornflour and mix into the meat until it's absorbed. Add the tinned tomatoes, the tomato puree, the sugar and the stock and season again, then transfer to the slow cooker with the meat, and cook on low for 8 hours. Add a dollop of crème fraîche / Greek yoghurt or sour cream when served. Serve with rice, pasta, or potatoes.

GOULASH

LAMB IN RED WINE, GARLIC, THYME AND ROSEMARY GRAVY

Lamb In Red Wine, Garlic, Thyme, And Rosemary Gravy, With Cheese And Chive Mash And Broccoli (GLUTEN FREE)

Lamb is unquestionably one of James' favourites, and I think he'd happily eat this every day ...Difficulty 4/10

Best in a slow cooker
Ingredients:
4 lamb loin steaks
6 cloves garlic
1 onion, finely chopped
2 stems rosemary
10 stems thyme leaves
200ml red wine
300ml strong lamb stock (2 lamb stock cubes)
1 tbsp cornflour blended in a little water
salt and pepper
1 head broccoli
To make the mash:
600g potatoes
handful of chopped chives
2 tbsp crème fraîche
150g grated red cheese, such as Red Leicester
splash of milk
salt

Brown the seasoned lamb and add to the slow cooker. In the same pan, caramelise the onion and add that to the slow cooker.

Chop the garlic, thyme and rosemary and add to the slow cooker, along with the red wine and seasoning. Add the blended cornflour and stir in. Cook for 7 hours on low.

To make the mash: boil around 600g potatoes and mash. Stir in a large handful of chopped chives, 2 tbsp crème fraîche, 150g grated red cheese, such as Red Leicester, and a little milk, plus salt.

Serve the lamb with the mash and steamed broccoli.

Lamb Tikka (GLUTEN FREE)
I can't tell you how tasty this one is (my mum taught me it's rude to speak with your mouth full). So simple to prepare, and uses neck of lamb - a cheaper cut, but one that is perfect for this. You can make your own tikka paste with garlic and the spices below or use the easy version which is just tikka paste from a jar. Difficulty 6/10

Our testers said: "Okay. Yes. This takes time. But blimmineck is it worth it. The blend of spices and the slow cooking make for a really authentic Indian meal... wayyyyy better than out of a jar. A lot of Indian dishes involve potatoes - why not this one to replace the lamb for vegetarians?
Experimenting with the colourings for the rice was great fun as well."

Best in a slow cooker
Ingredients:
cubed neck of lamb - 4 neck fillets
20g butter
1 tin chopped tomatoes
1 bay leaf
200 ml plain yoghurt
100 ml cream
Sugar to taste (optional)
1 tsp lemon juice
salt and pepper to taste
food colouring (optional)
75ml vegetable oil
For the tikka paste, blend:
2 tsp coriander powder
2 tsp cumin powder
1 tsp garlic powder (or 3 fresh cloves)
2 tsp paprika
1 tsp garam masala
knob of fresh ginger root
1/2 tsp chilli powder (more if you like it hot)
1/2 tsp turmeric

Brown the neck of lamb in the butter then add a couple of tablespoons of the tikka paste to the pan. After cooking for a couple more minutes, add the whole lot to the slow cooker with the tin of chopped tomatoes, 1 bay leaf, 200ml yoghurt, lemon and salt and pepper.

Cook on low for 6 hours then add 100ml cream and cook for another 30 mins or so.

Taste before serving and season with more salt if needed, or a little sugar if it needs a touch of sweetness - you shouldn't need any more than a teaspoon.

To make rainbow rice to go with this, cook your rice then take 3 tablespoons out of it and divide that between 3 dishes with a tiny bit of food colouring in each one (maybe 1/4 teaspoon) mixed with some water (about half a teaspoon - don't get it too wet). Coat the rice with the colour then fold it back into the uncoloured rice.

LAMB TIKKA

Lancashire Hotpot (GLUTEN FREE)

Being a born and bred Lancashire Lass, I had to include this one! Fun Fact - when James worked for Pickfords Removals many years ago, he met and moved 'Betty Turpin' of Coronation Street's 'Betty's Hotpot' fame! Difficulty 6/10

Best in a slow cooker
Ingredients
500g diced lamb
1 tbsp oil
1 onion chopped finely
2 sticks celery chopped finely
1 carrot chopped finely
100g swede chopped finely
3 cloves garlic chopped finely
50ml dry sherry
600ml beef/ lamb stock (1 cube of each)
good splash Worcester sauce
1/2 teaspoon Dijon mustard
pinch of nutmeg
3-4 medium potatoes peeled and sliced into thin rounds
handful chopped rosemary
handful chopped thyme
1 tbsp cornflour
2 tsp butter or butter spray
salt and pepper to taste

Brown the lamb, onion, swede, celery, carrot, and garlic. Add the chopped herbs, nutmeg, and the Sherry. Add the cornflour and stir until absorbed. Gradually add the stock, Worcester sauce and mustard. Taste and season.

Transfer to the slow cooker and top with the sliced potatoes. Top the potatoes with flecks of butter, or butter spray, and salt and pepper.

Cook on low for 7 hours. Finish by flashing the pot under a hot grill to brown and crisp the potato. Serve with a crusty roll.

LANCASHIRE HOTPOT

Moussaka (GLUTEN FREE)

I really love Moussaka - it's probably my favourite dish after Spaghetti Carbonara. I just love the slightly-thicker-than-a-lasagne topping, and the cinnamon undertones. Just delicious. I have stipulated 500g of mince for this recipe, but I do reserve around 2/3 of that once it's browned for cottage pies or whatever the following day, so adjust accordingly This will easily serve 4. It's a bit more time consuming, but it's worth it! Difficulty 7/10

Our testers said: "Beautiful. Just beautiful. Don't want to sound like I'm sucking up... but BEAUTIFUL!"

Ingredients:
500g minced lamb
1 tbsp oil
1 onion chopped finely
3 cloves garlic chopped finely
1 400g tin chopped tomatoes
2 tbsp tomato puree
50ml dry sherry
50ml red wine
600ml beef/ lamb stock (1 cube of each)
good splash Worcester sauce
1/2 tsp Dijon mustard
Pinch nutmeg
2-3 medium potatoes peeled and sliced into thin rounds
2 large aubergines sliced longways, thinly
1 tbsp cornflour
2 tsp butter or butter spray
salt and pepper to taste
For the béchamel sauce:
400ml milk
1 tbsp butter
1 tbsp cornflour
1/4 teaspoon nutmeg
200g grated cheese and more for sprinkling
2 egg yolks, whisked.

Preheat the oven to 200°C. Salt the aubergines (lay them on a tray and sprinkle liberally with salt) while you make the meat sauce - this is to draw out the moisture and any bitterness. Fry the lamb, onions, herbs, and garlic - then remove 2/3 of this mixture and put that straight in the fridge for tomorrow. To the remainder, add the cinnamon and wine, then the stock, tomatoes, and puree. It will be very liquid at this stage - it wants to cook down for 20-30 minutes until it resembles Bolognese sauce - then remove the cinnamon stick.

Pat the aubergines dry. If you have a skillet pan, use it to cook the aubergines to get the nice, charred lines on them. Otherwise grill or fry them until they get a bit of colour on each side. Do the same with the sliced potatoes.

I use the 'all in one method' for the béchamel sauce, but you can do it as a roux. Put the milk, butter and flour in a saucepan and heat and stir until you have a thick white sauce. Add the nutmeg then the cheese. Taste and season with salt. Take it off the heat and allow it to cool for a bit. When it has cooled sufficiently, add some black pepper, and mix in the two egg yolks (you don't want them to cook or scramble before it goes into the oven, so the béchamel wants to be lukewarm).

Layer the different elements in the dish: first the potatoes, then a sprinkle of cheese, next the meat sauce and a little more cheese, then the aubergine, and finally the béchamel.

Sprinkle more cheese on the top. Bake for around 30-40 minutes and allow it to rest for at least half an hour before you try to cut it. This is really delicious with some garlic bread.

MOUSSAKA

Pork Loin in Cider, Sage, and Wholegrain Mustard Sauce (GLUTEN FREE)
Pork loin chops have a sentimental place in my heart - my youngest used to refer to them as pork 'lion' chops, so pork lion chops they will always be to me... Serve with broccoli and sweet potato fries. Difficulty 4/10

Our testers said: "I served this with a sweet potato mash and some sauteed broccolini. I even fried a couple of sage leaves in butter before making the sauce so I would have a fancy garnish."

Ingredients:
4 pork loin chops
250ml cider
250ml chicken stock
2 tsp chopped, fresh sage
1 onion, chopped
250g mushrooms, chopped
2 tsp whole grain mustard
4 tbsp double cream

Fry the onions, mushrooms and sage in a little butter or oil. Add the cider and simmer to reduce the volume by around 2/3. Add the stock and the mustard and reduce again by half. Stir in the cream. Taste and season with salt. Grill the pork chops and serve with veg/potatoes/sweet potatoes - whatever you like! Spoon the sauce over the pork. Yum!

PORK IN CIDER, SAGE AND MUSTARD

Pork Loin in Sage, Onion, and Apple Sauce (GLUTEN FREE)

This is literally 5 mins prep and then it goes in the oven at 180°C for 30 mins. It was very much a made-up-on-the-spot one, but I knew these flavours went really well together. Difficulty 4/10

Ingredients:
500g pork loin fillet
handful of fresh sage leaves (about 12-14)
1 onion
2 tbsp apple sauce
1 tsp salt
1 tbsp brandy (optional)
salt and pepper to season
root vegetables of your choice
for the vegetables, blend:
1 tsp of juniper berries
1 tsp fennel seeds
1/2 tsp coriander seeds
1/2 tsp cloves
1 tsp mustard seeds

Preheat the oven to 200°C. Season and sear the pork in a hot pan. Set aside.

Blend the onion, sage, brandy, salt, and apple sauce until you have a paste. Coat the seared pork with the paste and set aside until it is ready to cook.

You can serve this with roasted root vegetables. To make this, I spray chopped vegetables (diced sweet potato, swede, carrots, and parsnips) with oil and shake them in the spices. They are baked for an hour.

For the sauce, I just add a bit of chicken stock to the juices in the pork dish when the pork is done, and 3 tablespoons of double cream.

Turn down the heat to 180°C and roast the pork for 30 minutes or until cooked through.

PORK IN SAGE, ONION, AND APPLE SAUCE

Posh Lasagne (CAN BE GLUTEN FREE)
Posh because it contains bacon and Marsala! Different recipe from the veggie one (apart from the obvious meat instead of veg). Substitute for Gluten Free lasagne sheets if desired.
Difficulty 6/10

Our testers said: "The Marsala, plus the bacon and smoked paprika all make this dish really special. Everyone took seconds."

Ingredients:
500g minced beef
1 onion
handful basil, chopped finely
1 beef stock cube
50 ml Marsala wine
4 rashers smoked bacon - chopped
1 tsp smoked paprika
1400g tin chopped tomatoes
1 tbsp tomato puree
1 tbsp butter
1 tbsp cornflour
500ml milk
nutmeg
salt and pepper
300g cheese (Cheddar)
75g Parmesan grated
3 tbsp double cream

Preheat the oven to 180°C. Brown the onions, bacon, and minced beef. Add the smoked paprika, stock cube then the Marsala. Stir in the basil and add the tomatoes, tomato puree and salt and pepper. Put the milk, butter and cornflour in a saucepan and heat and stir until it becomes a thick sauce. Add nutmeg, salt, and pepper to taste. Add 2/3 of the cheese and stir until melted. Add the cream. Mix the remaining third of the cheese with the Parmesan. Spread half of the meat mixture in an oven dish. Layer with lasagne sheets. Add half the béchamel/ cheese sauce and another layer of lasagne sheets. Add the remainder of the meat sauce and a final layer of lasagne sheets. Finally, add the remaining béchamel/cheese sauce and sprinkle the rest of the cheese on the top and cover with foil. Cook for 45 minutes then remove the foil and cook for a further 35 minutes. Allow the lasagne to rest for 30 minutes before cutting and serving.

POSH LASAGNE

Sausage and Bean Casserole (GLUTEN FREE)
Smoky sausage and bean casserole. Rustic and super comforting. Delicious with a nice chunk of crusty, buttered bread. Difficulty: 3/10

Best in a slow cooker Ingredients:
12 gluten free sausages
1 onion, finely chopped
1 yellow pepper, finely chopped
1 400g tin chopped tomatoes
2 tbsp tomato puree
2 tsp smoked paprika
1 beef stock cube
1 tsp salt
1 tsp sugar/ sweetener
1 400g tin mixed beans
A glug of red wine should you be so inclined (I am so inclined) and/or 200ml water

Brown the sausages and set aside. Brown the onion and yellow pepper. Add the smoked paprika and the crumbled stock cube. Add the tinned tomatoes, beans, tomato puree, salt, and sweetener. Mix together then add the liquid you're using. Transfer everything to a slow cooker and cook on high for 3-4 hours.

Shepherd's Pie (GLUTEN FREE)
Traditionally, you should put carrots in a cottage pie, and it's a beef gravy...but as you've seen by now, I like doing my own thing. So this is more of a cross between a shepherd's pie and a cottage pie, and while I haven't included any carrots, I've mixed the potato topping with a different veg - butternut squash. I've also thrown a bit of smoked bacon in there too, because - why not! Difficulty: 4/10

Our testers said: "Before I could even open my mouth to ask my husband what he thought, he exclaimed "This one's 10/10"!"
Ingredients:
500g minced beef
4 rashers smoked bacon
1 onion, finely chopped
2 stalks celery finely chopped
2 tsp dried thyme
400g butternut squash
6 largish potatoes, peeled and cubed
1 beef stock cube
1 lamb stock cube
1 tbsp cornflour
2 chicken stock cubes
salt and pepper
100g grated hard cheese such as Cheddar

Preheat the oven to 180°C. Fry the beef, bacon, celery, and onion until browned. Add the thyme. Make up 500ml stock from the beef and lamb stock cubes. Add the first third of the stock and simmer let it reduce by half. Then add the second third and reduce again. Add the remaining third of the stock and then the cornflour mixed with a little water to thicken the sauce. Taste and season.

Divide the mixture between 4 small pie dishes (mine are about 4-5 inches across). Cook the potatoes and the squash in chicken stock. When tender, drain and mash. Season to taste. Top the beef mixture with the potato and squash, then top with the grated cheese. Bake for 20-30 minutes until the tops are starting to brown. I serve this with garlic green beans - it's perfect with crusty bread too...

SHEPHERD'S PIE

Slow Cooked Pulled Pork (GLUTEN FREE)
This one is a bit of a labour of love as it takes a couple of days in total, but it's worth it. James gives this one a solid 10. Difficulty: 7110

Our testers said: "It was really good with the macaroni and cheese. Another tasty recipe!"

Best in a slow cooker
Ingredients:
1 boneless pork shoulder
1 tsp cinnamon
1 tsp cumin
1 tsp turmeric
1 tsp smoked paprika.
For the BBQ sauce:
1 400g tin tomatoes
2 tbsp tomato puree
1 tbsp sugar / sweetener
1 tbsp white wine vinegar
2 tsp Worcester Sauce
1 tsp onion powder
1 tsp garlic powder
1 tsp smoked paprika
pinch of salt

Pat the pork shoulder dry and rub it with the cinnamon, cumin, turmeric and smoked paprika, before covering and refrigerating overnight.

Next morning, put the pork on a layer of sliced onion, which is just covered by chicken stock, in the slow cooker.

Cook on low for 9-10 hours and then remove the pork and discard the onions and stock. Place the pork back in the slow cooker and shred with forks.

Add all the BBQ sauce ingredients to the slow cooker and mix. Heat on medium for 2 hours. Serve in a bun with chips, fries, or sweet potato fries or wedges.

SLOW COOKED PULLED PORK

Slow Cooked Steak with Mushroom and Thyme Sauce (GLUTEN FREE) *This, for me, is pure comfort food - a slow cooked meat in gravy with a nice side of mash does it for me every time. Difficulty 4/10*

Best in a slow cooker
Ingredients:
4 rump steaks
1 onion finely chopped
6 garlic cloves finely chopped
handful fresh thyme chopped
500g chopped mushrooms
2 tbsp brandy
400ml strong beef stock
splash Worcester Sauce
1 beef stock cube
1 tbsp cornflour
6 tbsp cream
salt and pepper
oil / oil spray for frying

Brown the seasoned steak in a pan, then transfer to a slow cooker. In the same pan, brown the onions, mushrooms, thyme, and garlic and the extra stock cube - crumbled. When browned, add the cornflour, and mix until it's absorbed. Transfer to a slow cooker. Add the brandy and a little of the beef stock to deglaze the pan. Then add the rest of the stock and the 6 tbsp of cream. You can add a bit of gravy browning if you want it a deeper brown.

Transfer the liquid to the slow cooker, season again, and mix well. Cook on low for 7 hours. Lovely with a creamy leek, chive, and cheese mash.

SLOW COOKED STEAK IN MUSHROOM AND THYME SAUCE

Spaghetti and Meatballs (plus Burgers for the next day!) CAN BE GLUTEN FREE
This is a repeat of the Burgers/Meatballs recipe - but with the sauce instructions for the meatballs. Again - use gluten free pasta if preferred. Difficulty: 5/10

Best in a slow cooker

Ingredients:
500g pork mince
500g beef mince
handful thyme
handful parsley
handful oregano
2 tsp smoked paprika
1 tsp salt
1/2 tsp pepper
1 tsp MSG (optional)
2 tsp Stubbs Liquid Smoke
2 eggs
1 tbsp cornflour
For the sauce:
1 400g tin chopped tomatoes
2 tbsp tomato puree
1 tsp sugar / sweetener
1/2 tsp salt
1/2 tsp black pepper
1 tsp garlic powder
150 ml red wine
2 beef stock cubes - crumbled
basil - fresh or dried - to taste

Chop the herbs finely then combine all the ingredients together. Take out 4 tennis ball sized portions of the mixture and shape into patties on a floured surface. Shape the remainder of the mixture into meatballs - you should get 4 burgers and around 25 meatballs. Brown the meatballs and add them to the slow cooker.

Add all the sauce ingredients above to the pan and bring to the boil. Pour the mixture over the meatballs and stir. Cook on low for 6-7 hours. Cook the spaghetti and stir in a few large spoons of the sauce. Add the meatballs.

SPAGHETTI AND MEATBALLS

Special Fried Rice (GLUTEN FREE)
Special Fried Rice is a staple in this house. I love that you can pretty much put in what you've got in (within reason). Some of the pulled pork recipe would go very nicely with this rice. Very quick, very easy, but don't be tempted to save any and reheat it - not worth the risk. Difficulty: 2/10

Our testers said: "The name for this one is verrrrrry appropriate as it WAS something special. I added chilli to my bowl as I am a chilli freak. Shiitake mushrooms could replace the chicken and ham for vegetarians."

300g rice (and the same amount of water - I do mine in the rice cooker, but you can cook it however you like)
2 cooked chicken breasts
4 slices ham
200g cooked prawns
4 spring onions chopped
4 slices smoked salmon
handful frozen peas
1 tbsp vegetable oil
2 tbsp soy sauce
2 eggs
1 tsp MSG (optional)

Chop the chicken, ham, salmon, and onions and add them and the prawns and peas to a hot wok with the oil in it. Heat until piping hot throughout.

In another pan use the two eggs to make a small omelette and shred it. When the rice is done, add it and the egg to the wok and mix thoroughly. Add the soy sauce and the MSG (if using) and mix again before serving.

The MSG is what gives it that authentic takeaway flavour, but some people are intolerant to it, so it's totally optional. MSG occurs naturally in things like tomato, Parmesan, mushrooms, and soy sauce. The evidence suggests that it's safe, but totally up to you if you add it or not.

SPECIAL FRIED RICE

Steak Parmigiana (CAN BE GLUTEN FREE)
More often done with chicken or just aubergine on its own, but also yummy with steak. Use gluten free bread, if required, for the crumb. Difficulty 5/10

Our testers said: "Really tasty and full of different textures - Hubby went back for 3rds. Simply lush and not too difficult to make. "

Ingredients:
2 sirloin steaks
1/2 aubergine, thinly sliced
100g grated mozzarella
For the crumb
1 tbsp cornflour
2 eggs, whisked
300g wholemeal bread, blended into breadcrumbs
50g Parmesan, grated
1/2 tsp salt
1/2 tsp pepper
1/2 tsp mustard powder
For the tomato sauce:
1 400g can chopped tomatoes
1 beef stock cube
1 tsp garlic powder
1 tsp sugar / sweetener
handful fresh chopped basil
salt and pepper
1 tbsp tomato puree
50ml red wine

Preheat the oven to 160°C. Salt the slices of aubergine for about half an hour. This draws out the excess moisture and any bitterness. Place all the sauce ingredients in a saucepan and simmer until reduced by a third. Blend. Mix the breadcrumbs with the Parmesan, mustard powder, salt, and pepper. Dredge the steaks in the cornflour and then the egg mixture , and finally the breadcrumbs. Repeat this process. Fry the breaded steaks for a couple of minutes each side, to brown the breadcrumbs, then place in an oven proof dish and pour 2/3 of the sauce over the steak, topping it with the mozzarella. Cook for 25-30 minutes in the oven, to ensure it's well cooked (important on a neutropenic diet), but if you can eat it pink, it just needs 15 minutes. Cook some pasta at the same time. Mix the remaining third of the tomato sauce with the drained pasta. Dry the aubergine slices, then cook for 3-4 minutes each side in a griddle pan. Place the aubergine slices on top of the pasta, then the breaded steak on top of that.

STEAK PARMIGIANA

TERIYAKI STEAK

Teriyaki Steak (GLUTEN FREE)

Another fusion one here - and very colourful! Now, my steak is a little rare (I like it that way), but on a neutropenic diet you know by now you need to cook it so it's well done. Difficulty: 6/10

Ingredients:
4 steaks of your choice
For the sauce:
6 tbsp sugar or sweetener
70ml soy sauce
1 tsp dried ginger
1 tsp garlic puree
1 tbsp rice wine
1 tbsp tomato puree
1/2 tsp smoked paprika
3 peppers - red, green, and yellow sliced into strips
1 onion - sliced into strips
1 tbsp toasted sesame seeds
food colouring (optional)

Cook the rice and keep it hot (a rice cooker is ideal for this, or you can cook the rice last). Stir fry the pepper and onion before adding the toasted sesame seeds. Cook the steaks until well done and set aside to rest. Add all the sauce ingredients to the pan and heat until bubbling. Slice the steaks and spoon the sauce over the top. For the rice, add a little food colouring to 3 separate bowls, with half a teaspoon of water in each, and stir in a large spoonful of rice into each before mixing back into the uncoloured rice.

Toad in the Hole (GLUTEN FREE)
My eldest daughter, Becky, is gluten free, but loves Yorkshire pudding so I had to find a way to make a gluten free one a few years ago. My first few tries came out flat, but this one works. Try Linda McCartney red onion and rosemary sausages for this if you're vegetarian - delicious! Difficulty 6/10

Ingredients:
120g cornflour
3 eggs
200ml milk
salt
12 gluten free sausages
vegetable oil

Preheat the oven to 230°C. Fry the sausages until browned and set aside. Put enough oil in the bottom of an oven proof dish to cover it, and heat until it's smoking. Mix the flour, eggs, milk, and salt to make a batter - add an ice cube to it and let it sit for ten mins in the fridge. Put the sausages in the dish and pour over the batter - the oil should be smoking and the batter should sizzle when it goes in. Bake for 25-30 minutes, until the batter has puffed up and is golden brown. Serve with lashings of gravy!

TOAD IN THE HOLE

VILLETTA PIE

Villetta Pie (GLUTEN FREE)
A really nice recipe to do if you have made double quantities of Bolognese sauce. This is really my Italian take on a cottage pie - 'Vi/Jetta Pie', (Vi/Jetta means 'cottage' in Italian). I think we all prefer this version to a regular cottage pie, and it's such an easy one to make with leftovers. As long as the sauce is cooled quickly (get it in the fridge within an hour or so of cooking) and reheat until piping hot, it should be absolutely fine the next day. You could use 'Uncle David and Zia Paola's' recipe for this, or even my 'Posh Lasagne' mix, but you can also make up a super quick, very basic ragu sauce as below. Difficulty 5/10

Best in a slow cooker
Ingredients:
500g minced beef
1 thinly sliced onion
2 tsp garlic puree
1 400g tin chopped tomatoes
2 tbsp tomato puree
1 beef stock cube, crumbled
250ml red wine
handful chopped basil
1 tsp sugar/sweetener
salt

Fry the chopped onions and the minced beef until browned. Stir in the garlic and the crumbled stock cube. Transfer to the slow cooker. Add the chopped tomatoes, tomato puree, basil, sugar, and red wine to the slow cooker and stir in. Cook on the hob until the sauce thickens and the wine cooks off. Taste and season with salt, and top with hot mashed potato/root veg, before flashing briefly under the grill to brown it.

Fish

Cod Mornay (GLUTEN FREE)
We really enjoy fish in our house, and this is a really tasty and satisfying one to do with cod or other white fish. Difficulty 4/10

Our testers said: "Another very enjoyable and comforting dish and makes a nice change from pan fried fish. The fish was cooked to perfection. If allergic to fish maybe eggs could work? By putting the green veg at the bottom of the dish first, then cracking eggs on top and then covering with the sauce and cheese...? And for dairy free, perhaps replacing the milk with chicken stock and omitting the cheese, adding a bit of paprika and nutmeg to the sauce, replacing the Philadelphia in the mash with soy cream, then topping the whole dish with finely chopped cashews instead of cheese?"

Ingredients:
4 cod fillets
1 leek
400ml milk
1/2 tsp mustard powder
salt and pepper
300g spinach
8 large potatoes
handful of chives, chopped
100g Philadelphia or other cream cheese
250g hard, grated cheese (Cheddar or similar)
1 tbsp butter
1 tbsp cornflour
oil for sauteing

Preheat the oven to 180°C. Put the milk, butter and cornflour in a pan and heat and stir until thickened. Add the grated cheese (hold a little back to sprinkle on the top), mustard powder and salt and pepper. Chop and sauté the leek. Add the spinach and allow it to wilt. Place the cod fillets and the leek and spinach mixture in an oven dish. Pour the cheese sauce on top and finish with the remaining cheese. Cook at 180°C for 30 minutes. Boil and mash the potatoes, add the Philadelphia, chives, seasoning and a splash of milk and heat through. Serve with green veg.

COD MORNAY

Cod in Parsley Sauce (GLUTEN FREE)

A bit of a throwback to childhood tonight, although the original version didn't have any alcohol in it (and this only has a tiny bit). There's something very comforting about white fish in parsley sauce, and it was often what I asked my Mum for when I wasn't feeling well as a child...anyway, this is a more grown-up version of this comfort food!
Difficulty 5/10

Our testers said: "Alison mentions "comfort food" - yes there is almost a feeling of cleansing or healing when you eat this; a bit like being internally bandaged. Just a deliciously reassuring meal. Alison suggests mashed potatoes to go with this but as we had some yesterday, I made steamed rice with peas instead. For vegans... why not courgettes sliced lengthways in 1cm thick "fillets" to replace the fish and cook in the same way. Plus soy or plant cream to replace the double cream in sauce."

Ingredients:
4 cod fillets
large bunch of parsley - chopped
juice and zest of half a lemon
50ml dry vermouth
200ml fish stock
160 ml double cream
(I used Elmlea Double Light)
1 tbsp cornflour mixed with a little water

Preheat the oven to 180°C. Pan fry the cod briefly, then place in an oven dish and season with the lemon juice, salt, pepper, and 1/4 of the parsley. Cook for around 15 minutes at 180, or until the fish is cooked through.

Bring the vermouth to the boil and reduce the volume by half. Add the stock, and again bring to the boil to reduce by half. Add the cream and the rest of the parsley, then the cornflour mixture to thicken - I like this to be quite a thick, sloppy sauce, so it needs that extra oomph to thicken it up. It probably won't need any seasoning, but taste and add some if you want to.

Pure comfort food for me! This is best served with rice or mashed potato, I think.

COD IN PARSLEY SAUCE

Coconut Salmon Curry (GLUTEN FREE)

Another delicious one that's nice as a winter warmer. Not too hot, but bags of flavour from all the spices. Difficulty 5/10

Our testers said: "Flavour! Really tasty, this one. Vegans could parboil large potato cubes, fry them in a little sunflower oil, then place in the oven dish in the same way as the salmon

Ingredients:
3 salmon fillets
1 tsp ground ginger
1 tsp garlic salt
1/4 tsp turmeric
1 tsp ground coriander
1 tsp ground cumin
1 tsp garam masala
1 tsp chilli powder (optional)
2 tbsp tomato puree
1 400g tin chopped tomatoes
400ml Alpro coconut drink (use coconut milk if you prefer, but this works really well and is lower in fat.)

Preheat the oven to 180°C. Place the salmon fillets in an oven dish. Start by toasting the spices in a dry pan. Add the tinned tomatoes and tomato puree and simmer for 5 mins. Add the coconut drink a little at a time and continue to reduce the volume.

When you've added all the coconut and you have a sauce, pour it over the salmon.

Cook at 180°C for 25 minutes. Set the salmon aside and add a little water to the sauce to thin it down a bit. Taste and season if needed. Serve with basmati rice.

COCONUT SALMON CURRY

Cumin And Coriander Crusted Salmon (CAN BE GLUTEN FREE)

Of course, cumin and coriander is a classic combination, but have you tried it as a crust on fish? It works beautifully ...Source gluten free panko if necessary and substitute couscous for polenta. The couscous is nice cold the next day too. Difficulty 5/10

Our tasters said: "My husband gave this a new name when he heartily exclaimed that I could make this "Oriental Salmon" again whenever I liked! Scrumptious meal - the fine crispness of the salmon topping, and the crunchy contrast of the nuts in the couscous that looks bejewelled with the peppers... a delight for the eyes and taste buds."

Ingredients
4 salmon fillets - skin on
25g panko
Handful fresh coriander - chopped finely
1/2 tsp ground coriander
1/2 tsp ground cumin
2 tsp olive oil
salt and pepper
For the couscous:
100g couscous
100g chopped mixed nuts
1 red pepper - chopped into chunks
1 orange pepper - chopped into chunks
150ml chicken stock

Preheat the oven to 180°C. Pan fry the salmon to crisp up the skin then set aside. Mix the chopped coriander, the ground cumin and ground coriander, a pinch of salt and pepper, the panko, and the olive oil, and spread the mixture over the salmon. Cook for 20-25 minutes at 180°C. In the meantime, pour the stock on the couscous and wait for it to absorb all the liquid. Toast the mixed nuts and pan fry the peppers (you can add other veggies here, of course), until slightly charred. Mix the nuts and peppers into the couscous and serve with the salmon.

Fabulous Fish Pies (GLUTEN FREE)

*This is easily the nicest fish pie I've **ever** had. I saw it featured on a TV show many years ago, desperately tried to find the recipe, then played around with it a bit. I promise you - it's spectacular. Not that difficult to make, but a real show-stopper - great for a dinner party! If you like fish, and you only try one recipe in this whole book - make it this one! Difficulty 5/10*

Our testers said: "I can totally understand why this is your fave recipe of the book, Alison. We really enjoyed this one! Will try making in individual dishes next time I cook a "posh" meal, because this really is very deluxe."

Ingredients:
250g piece of trimmed fresh salmon
125g trimmed fresh smoked haddock
125g trimmed fresh cod
200g raw king prawns (fresh or thawed)
125g grated cheddar
400ml fish velouté, (see below)
mashed potatoes (see below)
3 shallots, peeled and thinly sliced
10g unsalted butter
250ml white wine
250ml dry vermouth
½ litre fish stock
½ litre double cream

To make the velouté
Preheat the oven to 180°C. Cook the shallots in the butter until soft, without any colour. Deglaze the pan (to dislodge any flavoursome brown bits stuck to the pan sides from the sauteing) with the white wine and vermouth. Boil and reduce to a syrup. Add the fish stock, boil again, and reduce by half. Add the double cream, return to the boil and simmer for 5-8 minutes to reduce to a coating consistency (thicken with a bit of cornflour in water if it's too thin for you). Pass the sauce through a fine sieve. Chill and cover with cling film if not used immediately.

To make the mashed potato:
8-10 large potatoes. 100g soft unsalted butter, Salt and freshly ground white pepper
Peel the potatoes and cut them into evenly sized pieces. Place in a large

saucepan and cover with cold water. Add 1 tablespoon of salt, bring to the boil, and gently simmer until tender. Drain the potatoes in a colander and leave them to stand in a warm place for five minutes to ensure that all the water has drained away. Mash well. This process needs to be done quite quickly while the potato is still warm. Return the mashed potato to a clean pan. Slowly beat in the soft butter and season with salt and pepper. Keep this hot until needed.

To assemble the fish pie:
Trim the pieces of fish, ensuring that any skin, bones etc... have been removed. Cut the fish into evenly sized pieces. Heat the fish velouté in a wide, shallow pan; gently poach the pieces of fish in the velouté until just cooked through. Remove fish from the pan and place in a pie dish. Drop

the raw prawns into the pan and heat for a minute or so until they begin to turn pink. Season to taste (I find it

generally doesn't need any seasoning). Add the prawns and fish velouté to individual pie dishes. Everything should still be hot. Sprinkle the cheese on top of the sauce. Add the mashed potato to the top of each pie. Bake in the preheated oven for 20-25 minutes until piping hot in the centre and the top of the potato has started to turn brown. The top can be coloured further if you like by placing under a hot grill for a few seconds. Serve with peas.

FABULOUS FISH PIES

Filo Topped Fish Pie (CAN BE GLUTEN FREE)
James says "they're full of flavour!" - and they are! Substitute for Gluten Free pastry if desired. Difficulty 4/10

Our testers said: "Very satisfying contrast between the crispy filo and the soft filling within. Smoked tofu and mushrooms would be a nice substitute for the fish"

Ingredients:
500g mixed fish (cod, smoked haddock, salmon)
1 39g sheet of filo
1 chopped onion
1 tbsp chopped tarragon
1 400g tin chopped tomatoes
1 tbsp tomato puree
1 tsp sugar / sweetener
150ml fish stock
salt and pepper
1 egg

Preheat the oven to 180°C. Brown the onion in a little oil. Add the tinned tomato and tomato puree. Add the stock and reduce. Blend. Add the tarragon, sweetener and salt and pepper to taste. Add the fish and let it cook until the colour turns from opaque to solid - i.e. just cooked.

Transfer the mixture into 4 pie dishes. Cut a slice of filo pastry into 4 pieces, then tear each of these pieces into 3 and scrunch them up. Top each pie with three pieces of the scrunched filo and brush with egg to give it a gloss.

Bake for 15 minutes or until the filo is golden brown and crispy.

FILO TOPPED FISH PIE

Herb and Caper Sea Bass (GLUTEN FREE)
We were in Edinburgh a few years ago and James had a herby sea bass and caper dish in Ondine restaurant (amazing restaurant - the food critic Jay Rayner was dining at the same time as us, so we knew it had to be good!). James said it was one of the nicest things he'd ever eaten. So, this is my version. Difficulty 5/10

Ingredients:
sea bass fillets - 2 per person
finely chopped mixed fresh herbs (I use parsley, dill, and tarragon - about a handful of each - but you can use whatever you like).
capers
seasoning
1 tbsp butter

Put some olive oil in a large frying pan and get it really hot to sear the fish skin so it's nice and crispy. Season the fish and sear it in the hot pan. When the pan releases the fish (don't force it, it will let go when it's ready), turn it over. Remove the fish and set aside. Add the butter, herbs, and capers to the pan - cook until sizzling. Drizzle the herby, caper butter over the top of each fillet.

HERB AND CAPER SEABASS

Herby Fish Bake (GLUTEN FREE)

We absolutely love roasted veggies, and they go so nicely with this fish recipe. The topping is a mixture of herbs, garlic, lemon, Parmesan, and yoghurt. Really tasty! I've used hake or cod but it'd go nicely with any white fish really So, this one is a real mish mash, but it tastes so nice! I change the herbs around in this one, but the combination below is a pretty good combination. Difficulty 4/10

Our testers said: "This is so simple and quick to rustle up! And a 9/10 for flavour!"

Ingredients:
4 fillets white fish
handful basil
handful dill
handful parsley
handful chives
4 tbsp yoghurt (NOT bio or probiotic)
100g finely grated Parmesan
zest of 1 lemon
1/4 red pepper finely chopped
salt and pepper

Preheat the oven to 180°C. Chop the herbs finely and mix with the yoghurt, lemon zest, red pepper, Parmesan, and salt and pepper. If the fish has skin, I fry it briefly skin side down to crisp it up. Put the fish in an oven proof dish and divide the yoghurt mixture between the fillets, coating the top of each one. Cook at 180°C for 20 minutes (check it's fully cooked).

King Prawn, Butternut Squash, Bacon, Spinach And Sage Pasta. (CAN BE GLUTEN FREE)

The different flavours in this one go so nicely together. Substitute the pasta for Gluten Free Pasta if required. Difficulty 5/10

Ingredients:
1 butternut squash
400g raw king prawns (fresh or thawed)
8 rashers smoked bacon
1 tbsp chopped sage
4 cloves garlic - thinly sliced
300g spinach black pepper
250g dried pasta, cooked and drained
oil / oil spray

Preheat the oven to 200°C. Cube the squash and cut the bacon into pieces. Place the bacon, sage, garlic, and black pepper in a roasting pan with a little oil or oil spray and cook for 30 minutes, before adding the raw prawns. Cook for a further 10-15 minutes, or until the squash is soft and caramelised, turning half way through. Steam the spinach. Mix the bacon, prawns and squash mixture with the spinach and pasta and serve.

HERBY FISH BAKE

LEMON AND MAPLE SALMON WITH MINTED PEA AND ASPARAGUS RISOTTO

Lemon And Maple Salmon With Pea, Lemon And Mint Risotto. (GLUTEN FREE)
Absolutely jam packed with flavour this one - a firm favourite. Difficulty 7/10

Our testers said: "As Alison says, this is jam-packed with flavour - aye, that it is! I know a couple of people who are allergic to peas; chopped and parboiled asparagus could be a good substitute. A really pretty and Springtime looking dish that makes me think of primroses!"

4 salmon fillets - skin on
300g arborio rice
2 fish stock cubes made up with 800ml water
4 tsp maple syrup
175 ml white wine
1 onion chopped finely
1 lemon - just the zest
handful parsley chopped
handful chives chopped
handful mint chopped
4 tbsp cream
150g frozen peas
salt and pepper
oil / oil spray

Preheat the oven to 180°C. Score the skin of the salmon, season and top each fillet with 1 teaspoon maple syrup. Sear the salmon skin side down first, then flip it over and sear the maple syrup side too. Transfer to an oven dish. Top the salmon with half the lemon zest and half the parsley.

Soften the onion in a little oil or oil spray. Add the risotto rice and cook for a couple of minutes until the grains turn transparent. Add the wine and let the rice absorb it. Then add the stock a couple of ladlesful at a time, adding more as it's absorbed. Stir continuously.

After around ten mins, put the salmon in the oven at 180°C for 10-15 minutes or until cooked thoroughly. Towards the end of cooking (taste the rice - when it's al dente - a little bit of bite to it - it's about right) add the frozen peas - they'll only take a couple of minutes. I don't like to add the herbs too soon as they can make the risotto a bit green, so if neutropenic I'd zap them in the microwave for a few seconds before adding them at the last minute. Add three tablespoons of cream, the rest of the lemon zest, and salt to taste.

Lemon Linguine with Smoked Salmon and Chives (CAN BE GLUTEN FREE)
A lovely, zingy, fresh tasting pasta dish for the whole family - substitute the pasta for gluten free if required. Difficulty: 3/10

Our testers said: "The simplicity of this dish is enough in itself Might even work well with smoked trout for cheaper shopping. Really quick and easy meal to make - go for it!"

Ingredients:
1 pack dry linguine - or enough for 4
1 sealed vacuum pack of uncooked smoked salmon (say 200g)
100ml double cream
100ml crème fraîche
handful chopped chives
lemon juice to taste
salt to taste

Cook the linguine and drain. Fry the chopped chives in a little olive oil until they start to lose their bright green colour (on a non-neutropenic diet I'd put these in fresh at the end, but we need to ensure they are cooked).

Stir the cream and crème fraîche into the chives (the crème fraîche adds a slightly lemony taste, but you can add a little more lemon juice to taste - a teaspoon or two). Slice the smoked salmon into thin, long strips and stir into the cream and chive mixture.

Continue to heat (but don't boil) until the salmon has changed from transparent to opaque. Taste and add salt if required (not pepper). Stir the mixture into the pasta and serve.

LEMON LINGUINE WITH SMOKED SALMON AND CHIVES

Mum's Cheesy Fish Crumble (CAN BE GLUTEN FREE)
This was a staple when my sister and I were children. Apple crumple? Pah! Blackberry crumble? Nope. This is the only crumble for me! Difficulty 4/10

Ingredients:
4 skinless / boneless fillets of white fish
half a small onion - grated
60g butter
120g flour
60g mature Cheddar cheese
salt and pepper
lemon juice

Preheat the oven to 180°C. Season the fish with the salt and pepper, and lemon juice and place it into a greased baking dish. Rub the butter into the flour, using fingertips, until it resembles fine breadcrumbs, then add the grated cheese and onion, and mix thoroughly. Sprinkle the mixture over the fish and bake until the fish is cooked and the topping is golden brown (about 30 minutes). Delicious with buttery mashed potato and greens.

Orange and Herb Crusted Salmon (CAN BE GLUTEN FREE)
Another version of the crust that goes so well with fish. This one is a surprisingly tasty flavour match. Use gluten free panko if necessary. Serve with sweet potato fries and green veg. Difficulty 5/10

Ingredients:
25g panko
handful tarragon
handful flat leaf parsley
handful basil salt to taste
zest and juice of 1 orange
zest of 1 lemon
3 salmon fillets

Preheat the oven to 180°C. Chop the herbs finely and mix with the orange juice and zest, the lemon zest, the panko, and the salt. If the salmon is skin on, flash fry it skin side down until the skin is crispy, then divide the mixture between the three fillets - skin side down and mixture spread on the flesh. Use your fingers to press it on firmly. Cook at 180°C for around 20 minutes.

Pan Fried Salmon with King Prawn, Smoked Salmon, and Watercress Sauce (CAN BE GLUTEN FREE)
I really enjoy this with pasta, but you could serve it with rice or potatoes and it would work equally well. Substitute the pasta for gluten free pasta if required. Difficulty 4/10

Ingredients:
3 salmon fillets (skin on)
300g fresh or thawed raw king prawns
100g smoked salmon, finely chopped
150g watercress - chopped
200ml chicken stock
100ml white wine
200ml double cream
50g Parmesan, grated

Preheat the oven to 180°C. Pan fry the salmon to crisp the skin and brown on both sides, then put in the oven on 180°C for 20 minutes. While the salmon is cooking, cook the prawns in the same pan used to brown the salmon, and then make the sauce. Pour the wine in a pan and simmer to reduce the volume by half. Add the stock and reduce further. Add the cream and the Parmesan, then the watercress, chopped salmon and the prawns. Reduce the sauce a little more and season to taste. Serve with pasta, top with the salmon, then spoon over the sauce.

Pesto Crusted Salmon (CAN BE GLUTEN FREE)
Yet another fish crust - I think this might be my favourite one. Again, source gluten free panko if you need it. Very tasty and extremely quick and easy. Difficulty 2/10

Ingredients:
40g panko
4 tbsp pesto
4 salmon fillets

Preheat the oven to 180°C. Mix the panko with the pesto and spread it on the salmon fillets. Bake at 180°C for 20 minutes. That's literally it.

Prawn, Fennel, and Spinach Pasta (CAN BE GLUTEN FREE)
A lovely flavour combination and another that can be easily adapted to a gluten free diet by substituting the pasta for gluten free. Difficulty 4/10

Our testers said: "Another easy yet tasty one"

Ingredients:
200g raw or thawed prawns
200g spinach
1 bulb fennel, thinly sliced (stalks cut off)
handful fresh thyme, chopped finely
1 tsp garlic powder
olive oil / oil spray
grated Parmesan cheese
salt and pepper
tagliatelle (I usually allow 3 balls per person)

Preheat the oven to 190°C. Put the sliced fennel, thyme, garlic powder and oil/oil spray and salt and pepper in an oven dish and mix thoroughly so the fennel is coated. Grate some Parmesan cheese over the top Just a dusting).

Roast at 190°C for 35-40 minutes, until caramelised, then add the raw prawns and mix in. Cook for a further ten minutes. Steam the spinach and chop. Cook the tagliatelle and mix in the spinach, then the fennel and prawns.

PRAWN, FENNEL AND SPINACH PASTA

Smoked Salmon Croque Monsieur (CAN BE GLUTEN FREE)

One of my favourite quick and easy ones: a variation on a 'croque monsieur', which is basically just a posh toastie with ham, but fab comfort food! You make a smoked salmon toastie (it works just as well with ham, bacon, or even mushrooms), then just top it with a cheese sauce. Use gluten free bread for a gluten free option.
Difficulty: 5/10

Our testers said: "Deliciously simple yet luxurious. I added dill to the sauce because

I love a dill/salmon combo. This could work with soy milk and hummus for the sauce and sliced avocado as a filling, for a vegan diet. I was a bit worried about the Worcester sauce in the béchamel, but it works really well and discreetly enhances the toastie."

Preheat the oven to HOT for the chips Ingredients:

For the sauce:
400ml semi skimmed milk
200g grated Cheddar cheese
plus any red grated cheese to top (e.g. Red Leicester cheese or Monterey Jack)
1 tbsp cornflour
1 tbsp butter
splash Worcester sauce
salt
8 slices bread *buttered on the outside*
300g smoked salmon
For the fries:
6 sweet potatoes
1 tbsp cornflour
1 tsp smoked paprika
1 tsp garlic powder

Preheat the oven to 190°C. Cut the sweet potatoes into fries and soak them in water for about an hour - this gets rid of some of the starch and helps them be a bit crispier when cooked. Dry thoroughly. Coat with oil, then coat in the cornflour, smoked paprika and garlic powder (mix this together). Bake in a hot oven for 45-55 mins.

Combine the milk, cornflour, and butter over a medium heat, stirring constantly, until you have a thick, smooth sauce. Add the cheese, Worcester sauce, and salt to taste. In the meantime, make 4 smoked salmon sandwiches using the bread, and toast them in a griddle pan with the buttered sides on the outside. Place the salmon toasties on separate oven proof plates and spoon the cheese sauce over the top. Add a bit of Red Leicester or other red cheese and put back in the oven briefly until it melts. Serve with the sweet potato fries.

SMOKED SALMON CROQUE MONSIEUR

Salmon With Tomato, Champagne, And Crab Risotto (GLUTEN FREE)
This one's a bit special - we've had it on Christmas Eve. Difficulty 5/10

Our testers said: "We all really enjoyed this delish meal. The risotto took a wee bit longer to cook than usual - possibly because of a thicker stock. 10/10 for flavour. I used dried basil plus a little fresh oregano as not the season for fresh basil here."

Ingredients:
4 salmon fillets
300g risotto rice
1 onion finely chopped
handful basil finely chopped
2 cloves garlic
250ml champagne/sparkling wine
2 tsp fennel seeds
800ml fish stock
1 400g tin tomatoes
200g white crab meat
3 tbsp cream (optional)
oil/spray for frying
salt and pepper

Preheat the oven to 180°C. Spray/coat the salmon with oil and season with salt and pepper. Cook at 180°C for twenty minutes. Add the tomatoes, fennel seeds, half the champagne, some salt and pepper and the fish stock to a pan and heat gently before blending. Then add the crab meat.

Fry the onion and garlic gently until it turns translucent - then add the rice and cook gently for 5 minutes. Add the other half of the champagne and let the rice absorb it. Now add the tomato/ crab/stock/champagne mixture to the rice a ladleful at a time, allowing the rice to absorb each ladleful before adding more.

Cook until the rice is just al dente, and then add the basil and 2 tablespoons of cream.

SALMON WITH TOMATO, CHAMPAGNE, AND CRAB RISOTTO

Seafood Chowder (GLUTEN FREE)

This would easily serve 5 or 6 so adapt the quantities accordingly Prawns and scallops don't work in this very well - they go a bit crumbly in the slow cooker, so if you want prawns and scallops in it, I'd pan fry them separately in butter, olive oil, and lemon juice and add them at the end. Difficulty 5/10

Our testers said: "This is something of a luxury chowder - the flavours sing of a starter for a festive meal. This dish is ideal for an evening meal - if your slow cooker is like mine you can make this before going to work, and it'll keep warm until you come back."

Best in a slow cooker
Ingredients:
1 onion chopped finely
1 stick celery chopped finely
2 bay leaves
1 tbsp dried thyme
1 tsp salt
400ml fish stock
400ml double cream (I use Elmlea)
3 tbsp cornflour
half a bulb of fennel cored and finely chopped
2 potatoes peeled and chopped
1/4 tsp cayenne pepper
black pepper to taste
4 skinless salmon fillets cut in chunks (I use two smoked and 2 unsmoked)
2 smoked haddock fillets
approx. 20 scallops
handful parsley

Just put everything in the slow cooker on low for 5 hours. Serve with crusty bread and butter (optional)

SEAFOOD CHOWDER

Smoked Haddock Florentine (GLUTEN FREE)
You can't beat a nice, cheesy Florentine, whether it's with eggs or, as in this case, haddock. Difficulty 3/10

Our testers said: "Perhaps smoked tofu instead of haddock for vegans, or allergy to fish. Pure comfort food and my husband LOVED it!"

Ingredients:
4 smoked haddock fillets
1 tbsp butter
1 tbsp cornflour
150g grated mature cheddar
30g Parmesan - grated
500ml milk
1/2 tsp mustard powder
1/2 tsp nutmeg
salt
400g spinach

Preheat the oven to 180°C. Put the milk, mustard powder, nutmeg, butter and cornflour in a saucepan and heat and stir until it forms a thick sauce. Add the cheddar cheese and stir until it melts. Add salt to taste. Next, pour boiling water on the spinach through a colander until it's all wilted. Let it cool and squeeze/blot any moisture from it. Get it as dry as you can. Mix three or four tablespoons of the cheese sauce with the spinach and lay it on the bottom of an oven dish.

Place the four smoked haddock fillets on top of the spinach. Pour the remaining sauce over the fish and top with the Parmesan. Bake for around 20-25 minutes but keep an eye on it as it can brown suddenly! We serve this with thin slices of fried potato.

Spiced Cod (GLUTEN FREE)
A bit of a show stopper once it hits the plate - full of aromatic flavours. Delicious with rice or couscous. Difficulty 4/10

Our testers said: "This is a really simple recipe - the "hardest" part is getting the spices ready! The coconut milk and turmeric in the rice was the perfect accompaniment to the spicy fish."

Ingredients:
4 skinless cod fillets
Spice mix:
2 tsp cumin
2 tsp coriander powder

1 tsp ground black pepper
1 tsp turmeric
1 tsp ground nutmeg
2 tsp paprika
2 tsp mustard powder
1 tsp ground ginger
1 tsp garlic salt
1 tsp garam masala
1/2 tsp curry powder
1/2 tsp cinnamon

Preheat the oven to 180°C. Combine the spices and rub them into both sides of the fish. Sear both sides in a hot pan and then transfer to an oven dish. Cook at 180°C for 10-15 minutes or until cooked through. Serve with basmati rice - I cook mine in coconut milk and lime, adding a teaspoon of turmeric for colour, and topping it with toasted almonds.

SPICED COD

Teriyaki Salmon (GLUTEN FREE)
It has a really satisfying sweetness to it. I don't think you need a heavily flavoured accompaniment with this one - plain rice is perfect. Difficulty 3/10

Ingredients:
4 salmon fillets, skin on
vegetable oil for frying
For the sauce:
6 tbsp sugar or sweetener (I use Canderel Sugarly as it's the closest to sugar and we don't really use that anymore!)
70ml soy sauce
1 tsp dried ginger
1 tsp garlic puree
1 tsp rice wine

Preheat the oven to 180°C. Score the salmon skin and brown in a hot frying pan, in a little oil, until the skin is crispy. Flash fry the other side to brown then put in an oven proof dish. Combine the sauce ingredients and spoon the sauce on and around the salmon. Cook for 10-15 mins, or until cooked through, at 180°C. Baste it then give it a final five minutes. Serve with rice and green veg and spoon the sauce on top.

Tuna Pasta Bake (CAN BE GLUTEN FREE)
When we were on our honeymoon in Sorrento, James asked a waiter if he could have a seafood pizza with added cheese. The waiter refused, saying "It is a murder!" Nevertheless, we continue to have seafood with cheese (sorry Italy), and it's lovely! Difficulty 3/10

Ingredients:
250g fresh tuna chunks (or one large tin of tuna)
400g dried pasta
200g cherry tomatoes
200g tin sweetcorn
1 tsp smoked paprika
500ml milk
200g Mozzarella, sliced or grated
1 tbsp cornflour
1 tbsp butter
seasoning

Preheat the oven to 180°C. Fry the tuna and the tomatoes in olive oil, with the smoked paprika. Set aside. Make a white sauce by combining the butter, milk, and cornflour - I use the 'all in one' method and heat it gently until it thickens. Add most of the cheese (save a bit to put on the top) and seasoning. Cook and drain the pasta. Mix the tuna, tomatoes and sweetcorn with the cheese sauce and pasta, and place in an oven proof dish. Cook at 180°C for 20 minutes.

TUNA PASTA BAKE

Vegetarian

Asparagus and Pine Nut Pasta (CAN BE GLUTEN FREE)
We aren't vegetarian, as the contents of this book demonstrate, but this vegetarian recipe is enough to have James agreeing that he 'didn't miss the meat I fish'. so that's a winner for me! Difficulty 2/10

Our testers said: "The Asparagus and Pine Nut pasta was dead simple and got rave reviews. I will definitely make this again!"

Ingredients:
dried pasta - I don't always measure it. A couple of handfuls each usually suffices
15g of butter or a tbsp of olive oil
250g asparagus, chopped
150ml vegetable stock
50g Parmesan and more to sprinkle on top
4 tbsp pine nuts
4 tbsp double cream

Cool and drain the pasta. Sauté the asparagus until it starts to colour. Add the pine nuts and brown them - don't take your eyes off them as they colour quickly! Add the stock and reduce the volume slightly. Add the cream and then the Parmesan. Mix everything with the pasta. Sprinkle with more Parmesan and serve.

Cheats' Fondue (GLUTEN FREE)

I think cheese is one of the foods I'd find hardest to give up, and although I'm interested in vegan cheeses from an ethical point of view, this fondue is relatively traditional, and deliciously gooey .. .Difficulty 4/10

Our tasters said: "We did this in our special electric fondue thingy - keeps it warm and oozy while you eat it. Loved the brandy and nutmeg in this!"

Ingredients:
140g half fat Cheddar, grated
60g Gruyere, grated
60g Emmental, grated
1 garlic clove, minced
150ml white wine
1 tbsp fresh lemon juice
2 tbsp cornflour
1/2 tsp mustard powder
1/2 tsp nutmeg
1 tbsp brandy

Mix the grated cheeses with the cornflour. Put the wine, lemon and garlic in a saucepan and simmer. When it's simmering, add the cheese a handful at a time and stir until it melts into the wine. Do this until all the cheese has been absorbed and you have a smooth sauce. Add the mustard and the nutmeg.

Serve with whatever you want to dip in it! Of course crudites, bread, garlic mushrooms for vegetarians, but we also have it with smoked salmon, minute steak strips, king prawns, mini roast potatoes, and chicken thighs. Bacon and broccoli are also nice dippers.

CHEATS' FONDUE

Cheats' Pizza (CAN BE GLUTEN FREE)
Your kids will love these, I promise! Another of my super-fast dinners - and this one is so simple I'm almost embarrassed...but I have to share it because it's delicious! There is a story behind this one. When James and I were on honeymoon, we took a trip to Capri and had the most delicious, super-thin pizzas ever - they were out of this world. These pizzas are the cheats' version! For gluten free, just use wheat-free corn tortillas. Difficulty 1/10

All you need is:
A pack of tortilla wraps
tomato sauce (homemade or shop bought - enough to cover the bases) grated cheese to taste (Mozzarella is recommended)
drizzle some basil oil on the top.

First, you really need to lightly grill the tortillas on each side, otherwise they will be too floppy to hold the toppings. Get them just starting to brown and puff up, as they firm up at this stage. Then add the sauce just two or three teaspoons per pizza is fine), top with cheese, drizzle on the oil and grill until it's bubbling - not too high a heat as you don't want to burn it. Keep your eyes on them every second - they can catch quickly. And voila! That's it! 2 small tortillas are enough, but don't be surprised if people ask for seconds!

Cheese and Broccoli Pasta (CAN BE GLUTEN FREE)
My original version uses blue cheese, but that isn't neutropenic because blue cheese is a big no, but you can substitute it for mature cheddar instead. If you're allowed blue cheese, and you like it, it's a match made in heaven...It's super simple and fast, but very, very tasty. Difficulty 2/10

Our testers said: "Wonderfully simple. Simply wonderful."

Ingredients:
220g any dried pasta
1 head of broccoli
200g strong Cheddar, grated (Danish Blue or Dolcelatte after neutropenia is over!)
4 tbsp cream

Split the broccoli into florets and boil with the pasta for the last 5 minutes of cooking. Drain. Add the cheese and cream and stir until it melts together.

Cheese X4 and Chive Risotto (GLUTEN FREE)
Again, you can't have blue cheese on a neutropenic diet, so I substituted it when James was neutropenic, but it is such a lovely combination with the blue. However, you can use mature Cheddar instead. You'll also need to put the chives in early on if neutropenic, to ensure they get

properly cooked. This is super comfort food - it's a big cuddle in a bowl! Difficulty 5/10

Ingredients:
1 tbsp butter
300g risotto rice
50g mature cheddar (use blue when not neutropenic)
50g Emmental
50g mozzarella
50g ricotta
1 onion
125ml white wine
handful chives
2 vegetable stock cubes made up with around 2 litres of boiling water
pinch saffron
seasoning

Finely chop an onion and fry gently in the butter. Add the rice and stir until the rice starts to go translucent. Add the wine and allow the rice to absorb it. Then add the stock a couple of ladlesful at a time, and let it be absorbed before you add more. Keep going until the rice becomes tender (about 20 minutes). Add the saffron and seasoning (and the chives now if doing the neutropenic version). Add each of the cheeses in turn and stir them in until they've melted. Add the chives right near the end if not doing the neutropenic version.

Creamy Spinach and Tomato Gnocchi (CAN BE GLUTEN FREE)
I always think Gnocchi is such a lovely alternative to pasta - little pillows of deliciousness smothered in a tasty sauce. I've yet to see gluten-free gnocchi to buy, but I bet it's out there - alternatively, you can make your own gluten-free gnocchi reasonably easily with mashed potato, egg, and gluten free plain flour. Difficulty: 3/10

Our testers said: "Alison's Creamy Tomato and Spinach Gnocchi is just delicious! The ricotta adds a lovely creamy effect without being too heavy, and the spinach gives off a tasty green flavour that enhances the thick sauce. YUM!"

Ingredients:
1 pack vacuum packed gnocchi
For the tomato sauce:
1 400g can chopped tomatoes (I really like Mutti tomatoes)
1 vegetable stock cube
1 tsp garlic salt
handful fresh chopped basil
splash of (vegan) Worcester sauce

2 tbsp dried mixed herbs
1 tbsp tomato puree
1 250g tub ricotta cheese
salt

Combine the tomatoes, puree, salt, stock cube, herbs, and Worcester sauce. Heat on low until the sauce starts to become smooth. Add the ricotta cheese and blend (I use a stick blender) until fully combined and creamy. Cook the gnocchi in boiling, salted water - it's very fast, 2-3 mins. Drain it and add it to the tomato sauce. Then add the spinach, a handful at a time, while heating and stirring, and let it wilt and be absorbed by the sauce before you add more - it can take a lot of spinach! Plate up the gnocchi and sprinkle with grated Red Leicester (or a different cheese of your choice) and flash under a hot grill until the cheese melts.

CREAMY SPINACH AND TOMATO GNOCCHI

MAC 'N' CHEESE

Mac 'N' Cheese (GLUTEN FREE)
This can easily be made gluten free by using gluten free macaroni. Another mid-week staple for us. This is the ultimate comfort food, I think, and a super easy one to do. Difficulty 2/10

Our testers said: "We really liked this recipe!"

Ingredients:
300g macaroni
500ml milk
1 tbsp butter
1 tbsp cornflour
1/2 tsp mustard powder (mix it with a little water - just a teaspoon or so)
1/2 tsp salt
good splash (vegan) Worcester sauce
200g grated cheese (Cheddar, Red Leicester, Gouda, Mozzarella, Monterey Jack... or a combination of them)
50g red cheese to sprinkle on the top
1 tomato, thinly sliced
1 tbsp breadcrumbs (I use panko, but whatever you fancy)

Preheat the oven to 200°C. Cook and drain your pasta. Put the milk, cornflour, and butter all in the pan together - heat while stirring continuously until it thickens. Add the mustard, salt, and Worcestershire sauce, then stir in the 200g cheese until it melts. Stir the pasta into the sauce when the cheese has melted, then pour the whole lot into an oven proof dish. Sprinkle the remaining cheese on top, then layer the tomatoes on top, and finally sprinkle on the breadcrumbs. Cook in the oven for ten minutes.

Mediterranean Pasta (CAN BE GLUTEN FREE)
Another quick and easy one which tastes more impressive than it deserves to! Again, switch the pasta for gluten free if you need to. I think the brown pasta adds to this one - it was inspired by a dish made by my cousin Viviana, in Tel Aviv 35 years ago. Difficulty 4/10

Ingredients:
1 aubergine
1 white onion
1 red onion
200g cherry tomatoes
200g crumbly cheese - crumbled (I recommend Lancashire here, and Feta AFTER neutropenia)
1 red pepper
1 yellow pepper

1 orange pepper
handful fresh parsley, chopped
handful fresh thyme, chopped,
handful fresh basil, chopped
1 400g tin chopped tomatoes
1 tbsp garlic puree
1 tbsp tomato puree
2 vegetable stock cubes
2/3 pack whole wheat spaghetti
salt and pepper
grated Parmesan to top

After roasting the vegetables, set them aside. Then, make a basic tomato sauce using the tin of chopped tomatoes, chopped basil, parsley and thyme, the stock cubes, a tablespoon of garlic puree, salt and pepper and a little water. Simmer to reduce the sauce and add half of the roasted veg (the other half can be used the next day if it is chilled quickly. Cold roasted Mediterranean vegetables are a nice substitute for salad). Finally, cook the spaghetti and stir half of the sauce into the pasta, along with the crumbled cheese, before plating it up. Spoon the remaining sauce on the top and around the edge. Sprinkle the Parmesan on the top.

MEDITERRANEAN PASTA

Mushroom Risotto

Who doesn't love a risotto? It's a firm favourite here, and I love that there are so many possible variations. This is another delicious one for vegetarians, and you can make it vegan by switching the crème fraîche for plant cream. Difficulty 4/10

Ingredients:
handful fresh thyme - chopped
2 litres vegetable stock
400g sliced chestnut mushrooms
1 sliced onion
2 tsp garlic powder
300g risotto rice
200ml white wine
salt and pepper
1 tbsp crème fraîche

Fry the mushrooms, onion, thyme, and the garlic powder, until browned. Put the mushroom and onion mixture in a large saucepan and add the risotto rice. Stir for a couple of minutes, on a low heat, until the rice is starting to go transparent. Then add the white wine and stir until it's absorbed. Add the seasoning and then the stock, a ladleful at a time (you might not need it all) adding more each time it's absorbed. It will take around 20 minutes to cook When the rice is cooked, add a tablespoon of crème fraîche, and mix it in.

MUSHROOM RISOTTO

Mushroom, pecan, sage, and ricotta ravioli
This one's a bit more technical, and to be perfectly honest I'm just grateful when they don't burst ...but there is a foolproof trick to that, and it's never let me down yet. You boil the ravioli in a shallow pan - as shallow as you can. So, a wok or a frying pan - either is fine. One for the vegetarians, and very tasty - sage, mushrooms, thyme, ricotta, and pecans go beautifully together, and the sauce has a nice bite to it. You should get 16 big raviolis out of this, and it's very filling.

- 4 or 5 each is plenty (James got six the last time I made it, and only just managed it all!). You could try gluten free flour with this, but I'm not sure how successful it would be as the gluten makes the dough elastic. Difficulty 8/10
Our testers said: "What an amazing dish to tuck into upon our return from our market. This one is our fave out of all your recipes!"

Ingredients:
70g pecan halves chopped
3 shallots chopped finely
3 cloves garlic chopped finely
150g chestnut mushrooms
1 tbsp finely chopped sage
2 tsp thyme
250g ricotta cheese
salt and pepper
200g plain flour
2 large eggs
1 tsp olive oil
1 tsp salt
150ml white wine
200ml vegetable stock
1 thinly sliced shallot
100ml double cream
2 tsp thyme
1 tsp chopped sage
30g chopped pecan halves

Combine the flour, eggs, and olive oil. Mix with your hands until you have a dough. Knead until it becomes elastic and will spring back when you poke your finger in it (about 5 mins of pummeling). Wrap in cling film and allow it to rest for an hour or two. Roll it out into thin sheets using a pasta machine if you have one, or a rolling pin if not. It needs to be thin enough you can almost see your hand through it. Fry the 70g nuts, the garlic, shallots, the chopped mushrooms, sage, and thyme until browned - allow to cool. When cooled, stir in the ricotta, salt, and pepper. Set aside. Brown the sliced shallot, with the remaining sage and thyme. Add the wine and reduce by half. Add the stock and reduce by half again.
Add the cream and heat until it's a coating consistency. Taste and season with salt. Place

teaspoons full of the ricotta mixture at ravioli sized intervals along one sheet of the pasta before topping it with another sheet and sealing around the mixture - try and avoid any air being trapped as this is what will make them burst when you cook them. Cut into squares with a ravioli cutter, or a knife, and place in boiling salted water for 3 minutes. Top with the cream sauce.

MUSHROOM, PECAN, SAGE AND RICOTTA RAVIOLI

PAULINE'S CHICKPEA CURRY

Pauline's Chickpea Curry
This is a very special recipe because it came from my lovely Mum-in-law Pauline, who is sadly no longer with us. This is always devoured and is delicious (or 'delicioso' as Pauline always used to say) hot or cold. Difficulty 4/10

For non-vegetarian readers, my daughter Becky says: "Try adding minted lamb steak on top with a yoghurt and mint dressing. The lamb, mint and yoghurt sauce really balanced the spices out. Very tasty, as usual!"

Ingredients:
1 400g can chickpeas, drained
1/2 onion - diced
1/2 142g tin concentrated tomato puree
1-2 tsp chilli powder (you can omit this - it's still delicious)
1 tsp cumin powder
2 tsp coriander powder
1/2 tsp garam masala
1/2 tsp turmeric
1 tsp whole black mustard seeds
2 cloves crushed garlic
2 spring onions (optional)
3 tbsp veg oil
salt to taste

Heat the oil in a pan until very hot. Add the mustard seeds, which should pop. Turn the heat right down and add the onion and garlic - cook on low until transparent. Add the tomato paste and fry until the oil starts to separate. Now add the turmeric, chilli, cumin, and coriander. Finally, add the chickpeas and simmer for ten minutes. You can add a little water if you want to thin out the sauce a little. Garnish with the garam masala (and the optional spring onions when no longer neutropenic). Serve with rice or naan bread.

Red Onion Marmalade and Goat's Cheese Tart
Super-fast, full of flavour - a quick, easy one if entertaining. Difficulty 3/10

Ingredients:
200g ready-made puff pastry
4 tbsp red onion marmalade
100g tomatoes, sliced
handful green and black olives
80g goat's cheese - grated or sliced
handful torn fresh basil
1 egg for glazing
salt and pepper

Preheat the oven to 200°C. Roll the pastry out on a floured surface until you have a large rectangle, around 30cm x 20cm. Score a rectangle inside the pastry, around 3cm from the edge. Use a fork to prick the inside of the rectangle. Line a baking tray with parchment paper and then dust a little flour over the top. Place the pastry on top. Spread the red onion marmalade evenly inside the rectangle. Place the goat's cheese on top of the red onion marmalade, and the tomatoes and olives on top, evenly spacing them out. Scatter over the basil and season. Use a pastry brush to brush the edges of the tart with the egg, and place in the oven for 15-20 minutes or until the pastry has risen and is golden brown around the edges.

RED ONION MARMALADE AND GOAT'S CHEESE TART

Spinach and Ricotta Lasagne.

Serves 6. This is my youngest daughter's favourite meal (as soon as I dish it up she's already asking for seconds). I think the key to this one is the nutmeg in the ricotta - adds a lovely depth. Difficulty 6/10

For the spinach/ricotta
400g bag spinach - steamed and drained with the water squeezed out
2X 250g tubs ricotta
170g Philadelphia garlic and herb (or similar - Boursin works well too)
1/2 tsp nutmeg
salt
For the tomato sauce:
2 400g tins chopped tomatoes
handful basil, chopped
1 tsp sugar/sweetener
4 cloves garlic, minced
2 tbsp tomato puree
200ml red wine
salt
1 vegetable stock cube
black pepper
lasagne sheets
150g grated cheese to top (Mozzarella, Cheddar, Red Leicester, whatever you like)

Preheat the oven to 180°C. Steam, drain and cool the spinach, squeezing out any excess water, and chop finely. Mix the ricotta, herb cheese, salt, and spinach together. Put all the ingredients for the tomato sauce in a pan and cook until the sauce begins to thicken. Blend until smooth and add a little water to thin it down - the lasagne sheets need quite a wet sauce to cook properly unless you're pre-cooking or using fresh (I use dried).

Line an oven dish with half the tomato sauce, then lasagne sheets, then the cheese mixture, another layer of lasagne sheets, and finally the other half of the tomato sauce. Top with the grated cheese. Cook for 30-40 minutes at 180°C and test the lasagne sheets with a skewer to ensure they're cooked through. On a neutropenic diet I'd serve this with garlic bread.

SPINACH AND RICOTTA LASAGNE

Vegetable Lasagne
I actually prefer this one to the meat version. You can use any combination of roasting vegetables you like, but this is a tried and tested version. Difficulty 6/10

Ingredients
1 red pepper
1 yellow pepper
1 onion
1 red onion
1 small pumpkin (or squash)
4 sticks celery
cherry tomatoes
2 400g tins chopped tomatoes fresh herbs
(I use basil, thyme, and rosemary)
2 vegetable stock cubes
1 tbsp olive oil
3 tsp garlic paste
175ml red wine
fresh or dried lasagne sheets
For the béchamel sauce:
400ml whole milk
2 tbsp butter
2 tbsp cornflour
pinch of nutmeg
300g grated Red Leicester plus another 150g for sprinkling
salt and pepper

Preheat the oven to 200°C. You can use any veg you like for this and it's a good way to use up stuff that's on the turn. I usually include aubergine and mushrooms, or pumpkin, mixed peppers, onions, red onions, celery, and cherry tomatoes.

Chop the vegetables into chunks and roast in an oven proof dish in a hot oven, with the olive oil, for a good hour, so they're caramelised. Then add the two crumbled vegetable stock cubes, two tins of chopped tomatoes, 175ml red wine and the garlic paste and seasoning. Next, reduce the oven temperature to 180°C, place the dish back in the oven, and let it simmer for around 45 mins to an hour. You can add a bit of water to thin the sauce down a bit as it will thicken during the cooking process.

In the meantime I make a béchamel sauce. I use the all in one method and combine all the ingredients at the same time with a whisk, heating and stirring until it combines and you have a sauce that's pouring consistency. You could just add a bit of seasoning and nutmeg and leave it at this point, but I like a cheesy béchamel, so I add 300g of cheese too - I use Red Leicester because I like the colour it gives it, but you can use cheddar or Parmesan, or whatever you fancy. If it's not cheesy enough, try adding a bit of salt - it really brings out the cheesiness. When the vegetable sauce is done, I layer the sauces alternately with fresh lasagne sheets (sometimes I make my own but mostly I use bought) and sprinkle an additional 150g of cheese on the top (béchamel) layer. Then it goes in the oven around 30-40 minutes at 180°C. Cover and let it stand for at least 25 minutes before serving.

VEGETABLE LASAGNE

Easy Swaps For Different Diets

The Recipe Calls For	Gluten Free Swap	Vegetarian Swap	Vegan Swap	Slimming Swap
Chicken	N/A	Tofu	Tofu	N/A
Beef	N/A	Mushrooms	Mushrooms	5% Fat Beef
Fish	N/A	Jackfruit	Jackfruit	N/A
Bread/Bread crumbs	GF Bread	N/A	N/A	N/A
Panko	GF Panko	N/A	N/A	N/A

Easy Swaps For Different Diets

The Recipe Calls For	Gluten Free Swap	Vegetarian Swap	Vegan Swap	Slimming Swap
Pasta	GF Pasta	N/A	N/A	N/A
Cream	N/A	N/A	Plant Cream or Soya Cream	Elmlea Light
Cheese	N/A	Vegetarian Cheese	Vegan Cheese	Eatlean or Reduced Fat Cheese
Oil	N/A	N/A	N/A	Reduced Fat Oil Spray
Butter	N/A	N/A	Vitalite or Other Plant Based Spread	Low-Fat Spread

Dry Weights

oz	spoon	cup	g	lb
1/2 oz	1 tbsp	1/16 C	15g	
1 oz	2 tbsp	1/8 C	28g	
2 oz	4 tbsp	1/4 C	57g	
3 oz	6 tbsp	1/3 C	85g	
4 oz	8 tbsp	1/2 C	115g	1/4 lb
8 oz	16 tbsp	1 C	227g	1/2 lb
12 oz	24 tbsp	1 1/2 C	340g	3/4 lb
16 oz	32 tbsp	2 C	455g	1 lb

Liquid Volumes

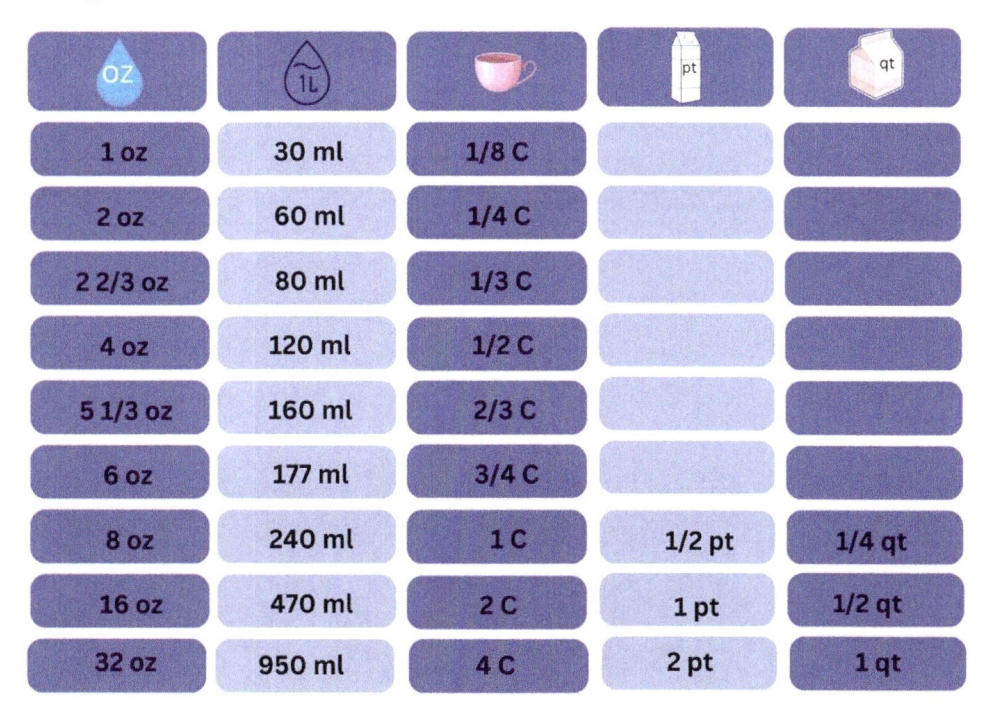

oz	ml	cup	pt	qt
1 oz	30 ml	1/8 C		
2 oz	60 ml	1/4 C		
2 2/3 oz	80 ml	1/3 C		
4 oz	120 ml	1/2 C		
5 1/3 oz	160 ml	2/3 C		
6 oz	177 ml	3/4 C		
8 oz	240 ml	1 C	1/2 pt	1/4 qt
16 oz	470 ml	2 C	1 pt	1/2 qt
32 oz	950 ml	4 C	2 pt	1 qt

UK Food Names v USA Food NAMES

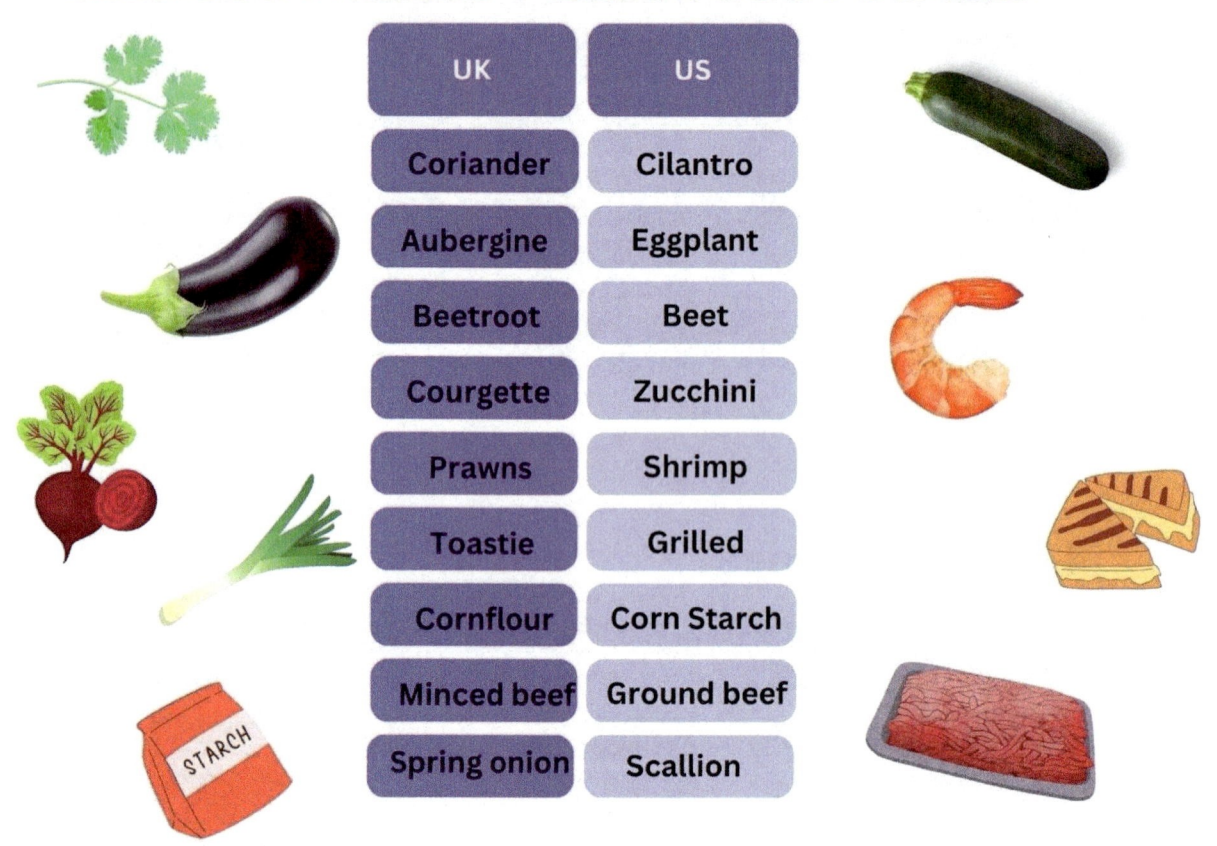

UK	US
Coriander	Cilantro
Aubergine	Eggplant
Beetroot	Beet
Courgette	Zucchini
Prawns	Shrimp
Toastie	Grilled
Cornflour	Corn Starch
Minced beef	Ground beef
Spring onion	Scallion

Notes

Notes

Notes

Notes

Printed in Great Britain
by Amazon